BUILT BY US
A Six Sigma Blueprint for Women Reclaiming Power, Purpose, and Process

Joy E. Mason

DEVELOP. NURTURE. ACHIEVE.

Denola M. Burton
info@EnhancedDNA1.com
www.EnhancedDNAPublishing.com
317-250-5611

BUILT BY US

A Six Sigma Blueprint for Women Reclaiming Power, Purpose, and Process

Copyright © 2025 Joy E. Mason

Portions of this work were created with the assistance of artificial intelligence tools for drafting and editing under the author's supervision.

All rights reserved.

ISBN: 978-1-967577-00-2
Library of Congress: 2025924335

Letter To The Reader

Dear Sister,

You are not just holding things together. You are courageously building them.

With purpose in your heart.

With power in your hands.

With process in your mind.

While others questioned your qualifications, you were keeping families afloat, leading teams, launching ideas, creating small businesses, and shaping futures.

Women have always built what we needed. We've built systems of care, systems of strategy, systems of survival, and we've done it with strength. They watch us and are astounded by what we do and how we do it. We wear multiple hats even when we are dead tired. This book is for that strength we all carry.

This book is a blueprint for building on your own terms. A reminder that your calendar, your boundaries, your priorities, your leadership—deserve structure, strategy, and soul.

You are not a predictable stereotype.

You are a brilliant masterpiece.

And no performance review, no biased policy, no unjust decision can shake the purpose and power rooted deep within you.

History has proven this. We come from women who refused to be broken:

- Fannie Lou Hamer, the determined Mississippi sharecropper turned national voting rights leader, reminded us she was "sick and tired of being sick and tired". After being severely beaten by authorities she still organized with unstoppable conviction.

- Grace Lee Boggs, a Chinese-American philosopher and activist, built bridges between labor rights and racial justice, proving revolution is both personal and collective.

- Wilma Pearl Mankiller, the first female Principal Chief of the Cherokee Nation, reshaped what tribal leadership could look like—with bold infrastructure, education, and health reforms.

- Dolores Huerta, a Latina labor organizer and co-founder of the United Farm Workers, coined "Sí, se puede" as a battle cry for equity and workers' rights.

- Claudia Gordon, a Deaf African-American woman and civil rights attorney, broke barriers in both law and disability advocacy, becoming the first Deaf Black female attorney in the U.S.

These women did not wait for perfect conditions— they built with what they had.

So must you.

This is your season to build systems that:

empower not exclude

uplift not undermine

propel not punish

build up not break down

solve not sabotage

You are Built By Us.

Believe in your brilliance.

Return to your purpose.

Design your systems-not just services, activities, initiatives or a luncheon.

As I tell my clients- You are the architect!

And keep building—because we need what only you can create, especially NOW.

With unbreakable belief in you,

Joy

Introduction: Build What Is Needed

This book is for every woman who senses that something is shifting and knows in her spirit that now is the time to build collaborative solutions and inclusive pathways.

I wrote *Built By Us* for the woman who sees the deep dark cracks in the foundation of our communities and our workplaces, and still dares to imagine what could be built in its place. I wrote this for the woman who has been underestimated, yet carries within her the divine blueprints for something bold, something better, something lasting, even in the face of the fall.

And the United States of America definitely feels like it is in a *fall*. The USA is cracking in ways we can't ignore, especially for women and people of color. Too much money and power sit at the top, while families at the bottom are crushed by rising costs and shrinking chances. If we don't rebuild systems that are fair and inclusive, we risk losing not just opportunity—but this country's future. Our country needs small businesses, families, women and women of color to thrive.

Here's a snapshot of what's happening:

- **Dreams of progress are fading** – In the 1940 birth cohort, about 92 percent of children earned more than their parents, but for the 1980 cohort, that fell sharply to just 50 percent, a drastic drop in opportunity. *This shows our education and job systems no longer guarantee that hard work leads to a better future.*

- **Middle-class share is shrinking fast** – Between 1970 and 2018, the share of U.S. income going to middle-class households plunged from 62 percent to 43 percent, a loss of nearly one-third of their slice of the pie. *This economic system has favored the wealthy instead of protecting working families.*

- **Wealth is slipping away from most** – Since 1975, nearly **$79 trillion** has been transferred from the bottom 90 percent of Americans to the top 1 percent. *Our tax and financial systems were built to funnel wealth upward, not spread opportunity broadly.*

- In **mid-2025**, approximately **300,000 Black women** left or were pushed out of the workforce between May and August—a dramatic decline that stands out even in headlines. During the same period, their unemployment rate surged to around 6 percent, nearly double the rate for white women.[1] *This mass exodus and rising unemployment are not just economic setbacks, they are alarm bells.*

- **The pay gap is growing worse for women of color** – From 2022 to 2023, the wage gaps widened: Black women saw their gap increase by 3 cents (compared to white, non-Hispanic men), and Asian women saw the gap widen by 5 cents. *This reveals how our pay and workplace systems still fail women, especially those of color, by not closing even small gaps in fairness.*[2]

These numbers are not just statistics, they tell a story of systems that are failing and a workforce that is shouldering the weight of instability. Black women have long been overrepresented in essential roles like healthcare, education, and public service—fields that sustain families and anchor communities. When they leave, it's not just an individual loss; it's a

---

[1] Joy Sewing. "A staggering 300,000 Black women left jobs or were forced out in 2025. Here's why Texans should care." *Houston Chronicle*, August 6, 2025.
[2] Center for American Progress. "What You Should Know About the 2023 Gender Wage Gap." October 22, 2024.

communal tremor, affecting schools, households, and the broader economy.

Yet even amid this crisis, resilience is possible, and already emerges from the smallest spaces. A neighbor supporting a teacher laid off. A local business amplifying a resilient mother's skills. A faith group organizing childcare. These grassroots gestures become the scaffolding for a stronger rebuild.

Collectively, we aren't just resisting, we are **constructing and we must accelerate building**. People are not broken. Systems are broken. Each small, inclusive act counters the pull of shrinking systems. And together, we're laying a foundation built on equity, care, and unshakable hope.

This is why I invite everyone ready to build. That's what I did. Not because I had everything figured out, but because I desperately desired to see change. I built the SixSigmaIndy Institute to give us what we are too often denied: the opportunity to grow, to lead, and *be seen* using our highest gifts and intellect. I created the very space I longed for—one where problem-solving and leadership aren't reserved for a privileged few, but are expanded to include those with lived experience, deep wisdom, and unshakable purpose.

And as you read this book, you'll see that the journey wasn't linear and I'm guessing your journey isn't linear either. There wasn't one moment, but *many* threads that God gently wove together. I watched my parents advocate with quiet, consistent strength. I endured a painful DEI training that left me more isolated than empowered. I had vivid dreams of problem-solving teams transforming our city. A friend invited me to write a Six Sigma article. And then George Floyd was murdered, and the world seemed to crack open. During all of that, doctors discovered a brain tumor that threatened the vision in my left eye. The tumor was finally removed in July of 2022.

Each of those moments was a seed. A nudge. A stitch in a much larger design. And eventually, I stood in the middle of something that had been forming all along: a movement, an institute, a mission.

So here is what I hope you take from these pages: *Build Now*. Take what resonates—whether it's a story, a lesson, or a strategy – and use it. This book doesn't have to be *your* exact roadmap, but let it stir something in you. Don't wait for permission or perfect timing and please do not wait to get another degree. *Build Now*. Define your process. Get down on your knees and pray. Gather your courage. Follow the whisper. And build what is needed.

While my story centers the Black and Brown experience, I know that our collective healing, growth, and power depend on rising together. To my White sisters, I gently challenge you to recognize that your liberation is tied to ours. We are still too separated. Now more than ever, we must build with radical honesty, shared power, and courageous collaboration. Let this book open your heart and widen your lens.

Because what we've been doing in this country isn't working. The cost of inaction is too high and the fall is already here.

So let us rise, not with fear, but with faith. Let us build—*boldly, wisely, and together*.

Table Of Contents

Letter To The Reader iii

Introduction: Build What Is Needed vii

Dedication xv

Chapter 1: The Spark 1

Chapter 2: Stepping Into Purpose After Corporate 7

Chapter 3: Purpose Is A Process 13

Chapter 4: When Vision Meets Equity 17

Chapter 5: The First Cohort – Mistakes, Miracles, And Momentum ... 25

Chapter 6: Creating The Blueprint – Growing The Institute 31

Chapter 7: The DEI Problem 41

Chapter 8: The Transformation Of Women Leaders 47

Chapter 9: Community, Connection, and Confidence 53

Chapter 10: Using Every Talent – A Biblical Reflection 59

Chapter 11: Trials And Triumphs – Leading Through Storms 63

Chapter 12: We Are The Architects – Reimagining Workforce Development 71

Chapter 13: Built To Last – Our Blueprint Forward 79

Appendix 87

Acknowledgements 97

About The Author 99

Index Of Terms 101

Dedication

To the women who are daring to lead,
the ones who have been overlooked, underestimated, and under-supported – this is for you.

And to Tony, my husband and safe place,
Thank you for your love, your loyalty, and your quiet strength.
You have been my anchor and my wings.
I couldn't have done this without you.

Chapter 1: The Spark

"We come from a lineage of builders—quiet revolutionaries who solve problems."

– Joy E. Mason

Sometimes the spark that lights your purpose doesn't start with your own story—it starts with your ancestors'. For me, that spark was my grandfather, Eugene Armstrong. My grandfather worked at Eli Lilly and Company, a major pharmaceutical company in Indianapolis, Indiana. He worked there during the Jim Crow era, a time when segregation wasn't just the norm in neighborhoods, but was also deeply embedded in the workplace. Black employees were often limited to jobs like equipment maintenance or animal care, while opportunities for advancement were few and far between.

But my grandfather didn't let those barriers define him.

One day, he noticed that the animal feeding system wasted a lot of food. The animals would toss food out of their cages, or it would fall on the floor, costing the company money. He proposed a new feeding method that dramatically cut down on waste by capturing the food before it could be spoiled or discarded.

The impact was so impressive that, in 1957, he was awarded a bonus of $6,689–one of the largest ever given to a Lilly employee at that time. His story even made the local newspaper. The photo shows my mom and uncle– just kids back then, standing in front of their brand-new house, partially paid for with that bonus check.

Today, we'd call his idea a brilliant example of continuous improvement and innovation. Back then, it was a quiet act of genius that helped build a legacy of possibility for our family.

From an early age, I was surrounded by problem solving warriors. My parents, both deeply committed to community advocacy, modeled what it meant to challenge injustice and strive for better. My dad was the Board Chair of the Fall Creek YMCA and served as president of the NAACP during the civil rights movement in Indianapolis. Our house was often filled with card-playing laughter, but it was also filled with conversations about policy, community, and protest. My-six-year-old ears may not have understood every word, but my spirit did. Those adult conversations at 422 Berkley Road became part of my DNA. They created a deep need for community connection and an insatiable thirst for justice.

That legacy of resilience and purpose stayed within me but didn't really blossom until I had seen more, knew more , and experienced more, especially in my corporate life. I spent over 30 years at Eli Lilly & Co., eventually earning a Six Sigma Black Belt certification and becoming a global change leader for Lilly's commercial microbiological and chemistry laboratories. My project manager role for commercial laboratories fueled and accelerated my passion for problem solving – especially complex problems. Whether it was streamlining lab management processes or managing massive regulatory implementations, I felt most energized when I was helping the work move forward and teams find their rhythm. It was actually a colleague who helped me recognize that navigating large, complex projects was a unique strength. My enjoyment for problem-solving and project management wasn't just about efficiency – it was about maximum impact. I wanted to see people and systems work better, together. Too often, the path to success feels uphill, lined with hidden barriers, tangled in complexity, and burdened by the weight of our own egos. So when a team crosses the finish line, aligned and victorious, it doesn't just feel like success – it feels like a miracle.

While working at Lilly, I had many successes, but I felt like something was missing. I didn't see people who looked like me leading, improving, and influencing at scale. When I started working full time in 1989, I was the only "one" in an exempt position in the Dry, Liquid and Ointment commercial manufacturing division. Sometimes, being the only one left me with crippling self-doubt, never feeling good enough. Yet the doubt was also the fuel that drove me to do my part to tackle systems, especially inequitable systems. I remember thinking: What if we took a problem-solving framework – like Six Sigma –and placed it into the hands of those who were ready to lead but lacked opportunity and access? That question never left me. It became a quiet dream, tucked between daytime hours at work, late afternoon hours volunteering, and evening hours focused on our two boys.

Looking back, I realize that I dreamed of teams – that solve problems. I imagined teams of women equipped with sharp minds, determined spirits, and data-driven tools, dispatched across the city to tackle education inequities, housing disparities, and healthcare gaps. This wasn't just an image; it was a calling. A glimpse of the kind of change I longed to see in my lifetime. Because when we solve these problems, we don't just shift the system – we save lives: more people get jobs, more families buy homes, more babies live, fewer men end up behind bars, and more people get a second chance.

I didn't know it then, but I was building a foundation for something bigger than myself. My professional training, my family's history, my faith – all of it was preparing me for the day when that spark would become a flame. That's why I immersed myself in learning, coaching, mentoring, and implementation. I didn't just want to solve problems, I wanted to empower others to do the same. And I didn't just want to tackle small, simple problems, I wanted big, ugly, complex problems. I wanted the problems people run from.

The spark that started with my grandfather's innovation in a segregated workplace grew into a blazing commitment to transformation. This blaze was finally triggered in 2020, when a Minneapolis officer was filmed forcefully pressing his knee down on George Floyd's neck for 9 minutes, leading to his death. Outrage over Floyd's unjust death was so widespread that protests erupted across more than 2,000 U.S. cities in the weeks following his death. Driven by feelings of helplessness and purpose, I founded SixSigmaIndy. Because building systems for process improvement, when placed in the hands of historically excluded women, becomes something revolutionary. It becomes a pathway to power, purpose, and lasting change.

> *"Process improvement, when placed in the hands of historically excluded women, becomes something revolutionary."*

Reflection Questions – Chapter 1: The Spark – A Legacy of Problem Solving

1. Whose legacy are you carrying, and how does it shape your leadership today?

2. What problems do you feel called to solve, not just because you can, but because you must?

3. If you could build a system; what would it be and why would you build it?

Chapter 2: Stepping Into Purpose After Corporate

"Leaving what is known is not loss—it is the sacred step toward becoming."

– Joy Mason

When I retired from Eli Lilly in December 2017, many assumed I was stepping away from ambition. Actually, I was stepping into purpose. I had spent decades building systems, leading global projects, and driving change from inside one of the most respected pharmaceutical companies in the world. I had learned what it meant to lead without all the answers, to manage resistance without giving up, to implement with limited support, and to thrive even when the spotlight didn't shine on me.

When the retirement package of 2017 was offered, several of my colleagues expressed that they weren't sure what they would do after retirement. I thought quietly to myself, "What would I NOT do?!" I felt an undeniable pull to use my experiences and my skills to build something of my own and deliver direct impact.

True to my nature, I had a plan. A year before retirement, I hired a business coach to help me prepare for what I called "Phase 2." I knew I wanted to stay in the space of process improvement, but this time on my own terms. I imagined helping nonprofits and mission-driven companies streamline their work, increase their effectiveness, and ultimately amplify their impact.

I didn't know how to sell my experiences and skills, so I hired a business coach. She brilliantly helped me translate my experiences and skills into services and products. She taught me how to build a business that embodied my values and my experience, through the name, logo ,and colors. She gave me the roadmap, and in January 2018, I officially launched Optimist Business Solutions. With the roadmap in my hand, passion in my heart, determination in my soul, and blind faith in my spirit, I leapt into entrepreneurship.

Building the business wasn't easy, but it was energizing. I created my own training materials, project templates, and consulting frameworks during late-night writing sessions that reminded me I was alive in a new way. The authentic creativity, intellectual stimulation, and the community connection that had slowly faded in my final years in corporate ,came roaring back. Within three years, I had a six-figure business and a growing list of clients that included schools, nonprofit organizations, state agencies, and the largest performing arts organization in Indiana.

I credit much of that early success to a mentor who offered me a piece of advice that still shapes my approach today. She told me, "Most consultants assess, train, and walk away. But if you can master implementation, if you can stick around and help them get the change done, you'll stand out." That advice became my secret sauce. I didn't just give recommendations; I stayed to help organizations implement the recommendations. Implementation became a superpower.

> ***"Building the business wasn't easy, but it was energizing."***

One of my proudest moments from my corporate life was leading a global regulatory implementation across more than five countries. The challenge was steep and the issues were complex. With a multidisciplinary team, I led the interpretation of a new international regulation and the development of a global strategy. I also led the implementation strategy. By the way, my manager was nowhere to be found. His lack of support was embarrassing and I was angry, very angry. I took his disengagement personally. But I rose. I am a "no excuses" person, and I apply that belief to myself. So, I had no choice but to lead from within, to manage resistance, align people, and deliver results. That extremely difficult experience was a game-changer. It burned away my doubts and taught me I could lead even when the support system wasn't there. And those skills, earned in the fire, became invaluable in my consulting work.

Entrepreneurship also reminded me how hungry I was to create and contribute. I didn't set out to build a massive business. But when you align passion with preparation, the results can be extraordinary. I found that purpose when paired with strategy and faith had the power to create momentum I never expected.

The transition from corporate to entrepreneurship wasn't just a career move; it was a reclaiming of my time, my talent, my spirit, and my vision. Now, I did have a stretch when I struggled to re-find "Joy". As I described in my first book, *Purpose: A Shift from Driving It to Embracing It*, retiring from Lilly, watching my youngest son leave for college, and turning 50 all happened around the same time. These significant events culminated in a brief identity crisis. Who was I? Even with the strong feelings of uncertainty and anxiety, I also felt a deep sense of freedom and limitless possibilities. In my professional life, I had finally broken free from rigid systems, competitive cultures, and the exhausting fight to be seen. This new found freedom wasn't just liberating; it was priceless.

Looking back on old emails, I realized that the young woman who softened her tone, worried about perceptions, and tried to fit in was mostly gone. Using softer words like *maybe*, *might*, *hopefully*, and *I think* to decrease the perceived "threat" had diminished from a flood to a trickle. Again, to regain my freedom and my own self-worth was beyond liberating.

I was starting to imagine and build something that reflected who I truly was, a problem-solver with a heart for justice and a gift for execution. Little did I know, the foundation I was laying would become the launchpad for something deeply impactful.

Reflection Questions – Chapter 2: Stepping into Purpose After Corporate

1. Where in your life have you been performing instead of truly thriving?

2. Where have you changed your voice and softened your tone to be accepted?

3. What would it look like to take one bold step toward the purpose you've been avoiding?

Chapter 3: Purpose Is A *Process*

"When the system isn't made for you, purpose becomes your process of reclaiming power, step by step."

— Joy E. Mason

I've always seen life through a series of steps. Not because I'm overly rigid, but because the process gives me peace. From a young age, I realized that I needed structure to succeed. Whether it was studying for a test in school, writing a research paper, or just preparing a plate of food, I followed a process. Steps helped me focus, helped me achieve, and eventually helped me lead.

I met my husband, Tony, in college (Miami OH University), and he jokingly recalls my routine: I attended class, ate dinner, took an evening nap, and studied for three hours in my dorm. This was my process for over three and a half years.

Even in everyday life, the process was sacred. When Tony gifted me a camera for my birthday, I didn't just pick it up and start clicking. I read the manual, played with the settings, took test shots, and studied the light. I experimented with angles, adjusted my posture, and eventually found rhythm. I also called my cousin for tips! That process, those steps, helped me capture not just photos, but memories. Every detail mattered. The more intentional I was, the better the result.

When I tackled complex puzzles, especially 3-D ones or those with double-sided images, I always relied on a clear process. I began by turning every piece face up, then organized the edges to create a framework, giving the puzzle structure before diving into the details. Next, I sorted by shape and color, grouping similar pieces to reveal hidden patterns. I built out sections methodically, and regularly stepped back to study both what was complete and what was missing, because the gaps are just as important as the picture. Solving the puzzle was never random; it was intentional. And when that final piece slid into place, it always felt like a miracle shaped by process.

This step-by-step rhythm followed me into my professional life. It's what allowed me to deliver results consistently and outpace expectations. I didn't rely on raw talent alone. I learned about the process. When others burned out, I broke things down. When others became overwhelmed, I mapped the work. I knew instinctively that excellence wasn't about rushing; it was about steady, intentional steps.

Over time, understanding processes has become my superpower. While we know powers and principalities intentionally put their thumbs on scales, seeing inequities through a process lens illuminates possibilities for small changes that can make big differences. Between my consulting work and the Six Sigma teams I oversee, there have almost always been opportunities to improve a registration, promotion, communication, compensation, hiring, intake or housing process. Focusing on the controllable parts of the process on a local level is the Institute's way of putting a thumb on the other side of the scale. "Process" may not sound sexy, but understanding processes can and does move the needle. Improving processes gives you the agency and the power to create change.

But here's the part that may seem counterintuitive: I'm also a woman of deep faith. Retiring from Lilly at the age of 50 was a leap into the unknown, a decision that made no logical sense to others. Some might say faith and process don't go together, but I've learned they do. In fact, faith is a process. It's taking one step without seeing the whole staircase, but trusting that the next step will appear. And trusting that it will appear on time, at the right time.

The Bible affirms this beautifully in Psalm 119:133: *"Order my steps in Your word."* Even scripture honors the idea that movement happens incrementally and under divine direction. I've come to believe that God honors the process just as much as He honors the vision. He builds capacity in the steps. He reveals wisdom in the waiting.

So when people ask how I built this work, how I stay focused, how I continue to create, I tell them the truth, my purpose has always been built one step at a time. Sometimes the steps were planned. Sometimes they were painful. But every single one was preparing me. Faith gave me the courage to move. The process gave me the map.

> **"Faith gave me the courage to move. Process gave me the map."**

Purpose is not a one-time decision. It's a daily process. It's listening, trusting, moving, reflecting and then doing it all over again. It's the quiet steps in private that prepare you for the bold moves in public. And when the process is rooted in purpose, the outcome always multiplies.

Reflection Questions – Chapter 3: Purpose is a PROCESS

1. In what areas of your life are you being invited to take a small but intentional step forward?

2. Where have you mistaken stillness for being stuck—when, in fact, God may be building your next step through the process?

Chapter 4: When Vision Meets Equity

"Equity is not a concept—it's a commitment to design a future where everyone has room to rise."

– Joy E. Mason

Some moments in history demand a response from deep within your soul. When George Floyd was murdered, it wasn't just a national tragedy, it was a personal awakening. I, like so many others, was grieving and enraged. But I was also restless. I wanted to act. I desperately wanted to move the needle – not just in rhetoric, but in results. At the same time, White friends and acquaintances started calling me, asking questions, trying to understand what was happening in our country. Their confusion frustrated me. I thought to myself, "How could they not see what we've been living with for generations?"

I was at a crossroads. The call to educate others on the root causes of the racial tension was palpable. Was I called to lead diversity, equity and inclusion (DEI) training? For two decades, I hated DEI training. Here's why:

I was just 24 when I sat through a diversity training that shattered my spirit and would negatively impact my corporate journey. In that training room, I saw the ugly biases that hide behind polite smiles and well-meaning words. I felt the quiet helplessness of seasoned Black employees who had learned to swallow their truth to survive. I witnessed the complicit silence of those who claimed to care but chose comfort over courage. And I felt my own innocence slipping as tears slid down my cheek, an open wound exposing both my hurt and my awakening. Those tears would dry, but the pain they revealed would harden into something deeper, tucked away for more than two decades. In retrospect, I believe the facilitators failed to establish the psychological safety needed for these types of workshops. Still, that moment planted a seed, a vision of equity that would eventually pierce through comfortable platitudes and cowardice and demand to be seen, heard, and lived. That moment tapped into a generational cry for justice that blesses and curses. That cry is embedded in my family's genetic makeup. It's a cry that does not and cannot rest as long as injustice prevails. As my paternal grandmother used to say, "What's in the blood must flow."

Because of that singular moment in my young career, I had intentionally stayed away from the traditional DEI space. My past experiences with DEI training had been painful. But I also knew something had to shift. When my business coach encouraged me to re-enter the DEI space in a way that aligned with who I am and what I know, something clicked. She said, "You don't have to do DEI the traditional way. Do it in a way that works for you and your strengths." That advice opened the door to possibilities.

That same week, a good friend asked me to contribute an article to her publication series about racism. I wasn't sure what to write at first, but then I realized: I knew how to solve problems. I knew how to use Six Sigma to break down systems, measure impact, and build sustainable improvements. So I wrote about it. I called it C.A.R.E. (Companies in Action for Racial Equity)—a framework for using Six Sigma to address racial inequities through action, not theory. Define the problem, measure the gap, analyze the root causes, improve the system, and control for sustainability. It made perfect sense! I saw how my professional toolkit could serve a deeply personal mission. Decades of learning systems, vision of problem-solving teams, the tragic murder of George Floyd, and my C.A.R.E. article were not random events. Even the pain from my 24-year-old self was not random.

Shortly after I wrote the article, I was introduced to a Master Black Belt Six Sigma instructor who shared my vision. He had used Six Sigma in nontraditional ways and was excited about the idea of training people who are oftentimes overlooked for learning and advancement opportunities. A series of divine connections brought this instructor to me. A colleague from a local quality organization connected me to a Six Sigma Black Belt coach; the Six Sigma Black Belt coach connected me to a Six Sigma Consultant; and the Six Sigma Consultant connected me to the executive director of a manufacturing training program, who connected me to the Master Six Sigma Black Belt instructor.

The pieces fell into place quickly, but not randomly. God had been planting seeds for years: through my work, through my relationships, and through my commitment to community. He had been ordering my steps. When the opportunity arose, I was ready. I raised $50,000 from four funders, all of whom trusted me enough to back an idea that had never been done before. That kind of belief is both empowering and humbling.

The Six Sigma Racial Equity Institute was born out of that faith-filled foundation. I built it with a vision that stretched far beyond technical training. At the heart of the model are three interconnected pillars: upskilling, building social capital, and negotiating one's salary. Together, these form the core of how we equip women to lead with confidence, influence systems, and advocate for the money they deserve.

Upskilling begins with the Six Sigma method itself. We teach participants to approach problems with structure, discipline, and data. These aren't just technical skills—they are leadership skills. They position women to be the ones who can untangle complexity, guide teams, and bring solutions that last. Learning this method not only elevates a résumé but also shifts how participants see themselves: as confident problem solvers who belong in the rooms where decisions are made.

Building social capital is the second pillar, and it is just as vital as the first. Advancement rarely happens in isolation; advancement often comes through people and relationships. That's why participants are matched with mentors—graduates who have walked this journey—and coaches, seasoned Six Sigma Black Belts and Master Black Belts. This layered support creates what we call the "give and get" model, where no one walks alone. Everyone pours in, and everyone receives. These connections grow into networks of belonging, affirmation, and opportunity, relationships that expand influence and deepen confidence.

Negotiating one's salary is the third pillar. Even with skills and networks, too many women, especially women of color, remain underpaid despite their contributions. We built negotiation training into the model so women could courageously advocate for themselves. This isn't only about money; it's about dignity and setting new expectations. When participants negotiate well, they don't just change their own trajectory, they shift the standards for their families, their workplaces, and the generations that follow.

Our three-pillar training is rigorous. Participants complete five full days of instruction, take an exam on the sixth day, and then dive into the Sherlock Holmes Six Sigma DMAIC Zombie Hunter simulation—a fun and engaging way to practice problem-solving. They then launch process-improvement projects with nonprofit agencies, gaining real-world experience over a six-month period. Their project journeys culminate in final presentations in front of their external project team, our board, their coaches, and me. I know this sounds like a lot and it is. However, when the participants present, their presentations aren't simply about accountability—their presentations are a celebration of courage, resilience, and accomplishment.

All of this (the pillars, the support and the final presentations) creates a circle that builds on itself. Participants gain skills, networks, and confidence. Mentors give back, guiding the next generation. Coaches invest their expertise, often for free or a small stipend, because they believe in the vision. Nonprofit partners benefit from fresh solutions to pressing challenges. What started as a $50,000 leap of faith has grown into more than a training program, it is a movement. A movement where equity is the center, where excellence and empowerment rise, and where women are reminded, boldly and unapologetically, that they were built to lead.

Our three-pillar model has evolved significantly since its inception five years ago, but it didn't look this way in 2021, when the first cohort was launched.

We launched the first all-female cohort through my for-profit business, Optimist Business Solutions. At the time, it wasn't an "institute" – it was a leap of faith. I didn't have a formal application process or a rubric. I simply reached out to women I believed in and invited them into something bold. The cohort included educators, fundraisers, IT professionals, and nonprofit leaders, women with passion and potential, who just needed a pathway.

The Institute was built to teach the participants Six Sigma and assign them to a project that focuses not on a manufacturing problem that would save money, but on a community or workplace problem that hinders results, impact and equitable opportunities.

However, vision alone is never enough.

Vision has to meet a process.

Vision has to be paired with strategy and support.

When vision meets a burning cry for justice, it becomes something catalytic.

Vision, process, strategy, support and the burn for justice guided each step. And it challenged not only the systems around us, but also the beliefs within us about what's possible and what can be built when our community leads with data, confidence, and conviction. I repeat this: This model challenges the BELIEFS within us – and our beliefs about what's possible. What we believe about ourselves and what we believe is

> *"What we believe about ourselves and what we believe is possible is our POWER."*

possible is our power. Our psychological, mental, and spiritual makeup allows us to build any system we want to build. There are definitely real and systemic barriers that make unencumbered "building" extremely challenging. However, I truly believe if women had to build a system from dirt and dust, together, we could because we have.

Reflection Questions – Chapter 4: When Vision Meets Equity

1. What vision do you hold that others might not fully understand but you know is necessary?

2. When have you let discomfort or doubt silence your voice in the pursuit of justice?

3. What is crying within you that won't rest until you decide to finally advocate and actively "fight" for what is right?

Chapter 5: The First Cohort – Mistakes, Miracles, And Momentum

"Progress is sometimes messy, miraculous, and exactly what was needed."

– Joy E. Mason

I still remember how the first cohort came together—the program was imperfect, unpolished, and absolutely miraculous. There was no formal process, no intricate application portal, and no sophisticated recruitment strategy. Just phone calls, emails, and the audacity of a vision. I invited women whom I believed had leadership potential but lacked access to the tools that could elevate their voice, credibility, and power. These weren't women looking to climb a ladder. They were looking to build ladders. Twelve women enrolled, and eight completed the program. The pilot wasn't perfect, but it was deeply powerful.

At the time, I didn't have an operations team, a formal intake system, a list of target competencies, templates, a learning management system ,or the project management system that I have now. But I did have an instructor with 30 years of Six Sigma experience and a deep heart for the community. He was the ideal partner, technically brilliant, a patient teacher, and fully invested in seeing these women succeed. I also had my dear friend and play sister, Denola. Denola was a Lilly retiree like me and she agreed to be the operations manager. Thank God for Denola– another critical piece of the divine puzzle.

I had an instructor and an operations manager, but I needed money to pay them. Again, with nothing but a vision, I reached out to my contacts whom I thought were value-aligned. With each contact, I shared my vision for leveraging Six Sigma for good. I'm not sure what I expected from those conversations, but they said yes. Each "yes" felt affirming and divine. With just less than $50,000 from my contacts and some proceeds from my business, I had enough to pay the instructor, an assistant, and my operations manager, and friend. We started the training on July 9, 2021. The participants ranged from degree to no degree, from corporate to grass roots, and from experienced to early career. This type of diversity was perfect.

We started during the COVID-19 pandemic so all meetings were virtual. The instructor had a slide deck, but the program did not have the curriculum, assessments, the participant guide, project selection process, project sponsors, or curriculum that we have now. These gaping holes should have led to a disastrous outcome, but it didn't. Again, steps! We took very small steps.

The women passed the exam, some on their first try, others after retakes. But passing the test wasn't the hard part– applying the method in real-world projects was.

One of the biggest hurdles was project selection. Coming from the corporate world, I was used to environments with structured processes, key process indicators, and accessible data. But most of these women were in nonprofit, education, and grassroots settings. The data wasn't always clean or available. The systems were often informal. It became clear that I was asking them to not only learn Six Sigma but also to master project management without the same type of support and resources that most Six Sigma Green belts in corporate settings have. Many participants got stuck in the "Define" phase for months. Looking back, I realize I expected them to run before they learned to walk. I made some mistakes, too. I sent late-night emails pushing them to stay on schedule. I called out delays in front of the group. I let my inner driver take the wheel, forgetting that transformation doesn't thrive under pressure but under care. It was intense.

> **"I was trying to protect the vision, but I was learning in real time how to protect the people carrying it."**

I was trying to protect the vision, but I was learning in real time how to protect the people carrying it. I deeply appreciate and honor people who agree to participate in pilot programs. Many mistakes are made during a pilot, but much is learned for the benefit of those who come afterwards. I now give myself grace. It was a pilot, and pilots are designed for learning. That first cohort taught me just as much as I taught them, and I am forever grateful to them for that.

Despite the bumps, the results were breathtaking. These women completed real projects addressing community and organizational challenges, projects that dealt with employee retention, resource access, and communication gaps. More than 87% of our Cohort 1 participants reported that they felt more capable of leading change in their organizations and communities. Several received promotions or pay increases. And all of them left with something deeper than a certificate, they left with confident conviction.

That first cohort also helped to refine the heart of the Institute. This wasn't just a professional development program. It was a transformation lab, a space for women to grow into the leaders they were always meant to be. It wasn't just about solving external problems. It was about confronting internal barriers: imposter syndrome, lack of confidence, and the long-standing silence around our brilliance. This program became a mirror, a megaphone, and a movement all at once.

We launched that first paper plane with paper wings and prayer. It wasn't fancy, but it flew. And it gave us the momentum to keep going. Every cohort since has benefited from the mistakes and miracles of that first group of brave women. They paved the way. They showed us what was possible. And they reminded us that when you plant a bold seed in fertile soil, it doesn't just grow: it multiplies.

The paper plane with the paper wings is a valuable lesson for all of us. Too often, we think the plane has to be fully built and ready to go. While the paper plane construction should be thoughtfully built, trust that it will evolve and be fortified over time. The anxiety-provoking experience of getting the plane up in the air gives you the information needed to make that plane stronger and better. When that paper plane comes back down, then you iterate and iterate.

Reflection Questions – Chapter 5: The First Cohort – Mistakes, Miracles, and Momentum

1. What past "mistakes" might actually be the soil for future growth?

2. Where do you need to give yourself more grace so that transformation can take root?

Chapter 6: Creating The Blueprint – Growing The Institute

"Blueprints build belief in what's possible and not yet seen."

– Joy E. Mason

The first cohort may have taken flight on grit and goodwill, but by the time we moved into the second year, I knew we needed a blueprint. We needed something more than vision, we needed more structure. I went back to my roots as a process improvement professional. I treated the Institute like a living system that needed feedback, iteration, and optimization. After every cohort, I collected surveys and data, held debriefs with coaches, and reviewed outcomes. Like a true Six Sigma practitioner, I wanted to know: what worked, what didn't, and how could we improve?

One of the first major upgrades was the addition of professional development days. Participants didn't just need tools, they needed the mindset and the muscle to apply them in real life. So we introduced new sessions: Strategic Leadership, Salary Negotiation, Financial Literacy, Project Management, and a Simulation. Each module was designed to bridge the gap between learning and application. These were the tools I used throughout my career, and now they were being passed on to women who were hungry to lead but hadn't been given a playbook.

Leadership development was a key area of focus. I was surprised when, after the first year, the lowest survey scores were in leadership confidence. That stopped me in my tracks. This was a leadership program – how could they not see themselves as confident leaders? Then I realized I had made an assumption: that they would naturally infer leadership development through the process of learning Six Sigma. I had not been intentional in helping them connect the dots. I adjusted quickly and brought in a phenomenal woman to teach strategic thinking and systems leadership. Her presence and expertise had an immediate difference.

I remember her analogy about car parts—how laying all the parts of a car on the ground doesn't give you a vehicle. Systems thinking, she explained, is what allows us to build something functional, purposeful, and sustainable. It was the perfect metaphor. I saw light bulbs go on for our participants. They began to understand that their projects weren't just about fixing isolated problems, they were about influencing entire systems. To do that, they had to intentionally build the steps, processes, systems, and ecosystems for real change. Building became the strategy. Reclaiming self-agency became the motivation, and Six Sigma became the method. With this powerful mix, building what we need overrides asking for what we need.

> *"Reclaiming self-agency became the motivation, and Six Sigma became the method."*

Too often, we get stuck with our heads down, working hard, and trying to make "it" work. In the process, we lose touch with the fire inside us. But that fire is still there. It's the light that knows how to build what truly matters, not from power or greed, but from purpose, talent, and shared humanity. Whether it's a real estate agency, cleaning service, wellness agency, hair care products, a second chance program, or the SixSigmaIndy training institute, we are the architects. We are the ones who can create something better. The blueprints are within us.

For many of our communities, the blueprint for "something better" has to include economic mobility. There were three moments that made this economic mobility focus crystal clear.

The first moment was early in the life of the institute. As a member of the American Society Quality (ASQ), I had access to their annual salary data. At that time, the ASQ survey results revealed that those who were Six Sigma green belt trained made approximately $10,000 more than those who were not. $10,000 is $833.33 per month. That's no small amount – $833.33 could go towards paying down a student loan, paying for high quality child care, contributing to a college account (529) or paying part of a mortgage for a home. The Institute could move the needle one cohort, one project and one $10,000 milestone at a time.

The second moment was when I met with a business man who appeared over Zoom. A mutual acquaintance connected us virtually. As the business man explained his model, I did my best to understand him, but he spoke and operated on an entirely different level. I was not intimidated; I was intrigued. When it was my turn to share, I described the Institute and explained its model which primarily focused on up-skilling. I also shared that the Institute was a new nonprofit. Without changing his facial expression, he made his dislike of nonprofits clear. He explained that people needed good paying jobs more than they needed nonprofit programs. His comment struck me, because he was clear and unequivocal in his distaste for nonprofit programs. Considering I clearly had a nonprofit program, I could've easily been offended. But I think I understood what he meant. He was trying to emphasize the need for robust pathways that lead to economic mobility. An examination of the research supports this urgent need. The research consistently shows that Black people have lower rates of upward economic mobility and higher rates of downward mobility.[3]

---

[3] Urban Institute. *Pathways to Upward Economic Mobility and Wealth Building for Black Women*. July 2024. Available at: https://www.urban.org/sites/default/files/2024-07/Pathways%20to%20Upward%20Economic%20Mobility%20and%20Wealth%20Building%20for%20Black%20Women.pdf

The root causes for the disparities are complex but I ended the conversation with the renewed conviction that I didn't want just another program.

The third moment was when I scrolled through Facebook one evening and stopped on a Facebook reel of John Hope Bryant speaking. I didn't hear the interviewer's question, but I recall Bryant saying that household wealth will reach zero by 2053 for Black people and 2073 for Latino people.[4] I was alarmed! When the business man spoke a few years earlier about his dislike of programs, I paused and took note. When I researched what John Hope Bryant said to the interviewer, I doubled my commitment with urgency. I had another data point that drove my commitment to help women leverage their new Six Sigma skills for greater economic mobility. I must help them get more money in their pockets.

As a result, we added a workshop on salary negotiation to our blueprint. The workshop was led by a brilliant female attorney and entrepreneur. Her session opened our eyes to the generational financial impact of starting too low on the pay scale. The wage gap isn't just about fairness, it's about tangible lifelong consequences. I offer my own career progression and salary over three decades as a testimony to the financial consequences.

For most of my years working in the corporate world, I was in the bottom quarter of my salary range. In case you're wondering, my performance reviews were consistently good to "superior distinguished". I did not know what others were making, and I naively believed that I was making "good money." So I kept my nose to the grindstone and kept working hard. I was unaware that my unjustified pay disparity could lead to a projected $800,000 shortfall in my Social Security benefits. That kind of staggering financial loss for myself, my family and others who look

---

[4] Institute for Policy Studies. *The Road to Zero Wealth: How the Racial Wealth Divide Is Hollowing Out America's Middle Class*. September 2017. Available at: https://ips-dc.org/report-the-road-to-zero-wealth/

like me doesn't just impact retirement: it reverberates through generations.

We carry an obligation to change that reality for others, even if it's one small, data-driven Six Sigma step at a time. We must equip our participants with the language and confidence to ask for what they rightfully deserve for themselves and their families.

Another adjustment to the blueprint was how we tracked outcomes. We started collecting data 12 months after graduation, pay raises, promotions, and new job opportunities. The stories poured in. Three women almost doubled their salary and attributed their increases to their new skills. Another applied and was admitted to law school because of her new skills. One of our alumni was hired by the organization that she was assigned to for her Six Sigma project. These weren't just incredible success stories; they were proof points—real world evidence. They validated the idea that when the disenfranchised are given elite tools and support, they don't just elevate, they lead. A handout, panel discussion, a workshop, or a 12-week program are appreciated but career elevation, self-efficacy, and more household income is transformative.

Our blueprint continues to evolve, but what remains constant is our commitment to continuous improvement. Continuous improvement for our program and for our participants' lives. We don't settle for good intentions. We pursue real results. And with every cohort, we refine our ability to turn potential into power and passion into measurable results.

Here's a shining example of a Cohort 1 Project:

> **Challenge**
>
> Black job seekers lacked access, encouragement, and confidence to explore careers in tech. Many didn't know where to look, felt they didn't belong, or didn't see themselves represented.

Goal

Help Black job-seekers confidently explore and apply for tech jobs by improving awareness, tools, and support at the start of their job search.

Process Name

Job Exploration Process

Project Summary

This project used the Six Sigma 'Define-Measure-Analyze-Improve-Control' (DMAIC) method to uncover barriers keeping Black job seekers from considering careers in tech. Surveys and interviews showed low awareness and lack of role models. Many didn't apply for tech jobs because they thought they weren't qualified or didn't see people like them in tech roles.

Prioritized Root Causes

- Lack of Awareness of Opportunities
- Lack of Encouragement
- Lack of Interest
    - Lack of Blacks in Tech Represented in Media (Shows and Film)
- Lack of Mentorship Opportunities
- Fear of Not Being Qualified
- Fear of Not Fitting into the Tech World

By following the DMAIC process, the team designed new ways to introduce tech early in the job search process. They created a Tech Careers Packet with job boards, starter roles, skill checklists, and salary maps. They also shared a simple "70% Rule", if you match 70% of the job description, go for it. The packet was added to the onboarding process for job seekers. Local Partners helped test the solution. Participants were also taught to link their personal skills to tech jobs.

Project Results

- Quantitative: 100% of program participants applied to at least one tech job after receiving the new materials.
- Qualitative: Participants said the new resources made tech feel "doable" and gave them the courage to try something new.

Our sample size may be small, but our DMAIC approach has the potential to increase the number of Black people applying for tech jobs.

100% applied and that's a start…. Applying! Earlier we talked about steps. The confidence to apply, even if the applicant doesn't have the experience, applying is the first step. What if a group could take this project, scale it and sustain it? We can move the needle, even as we navigate a hostile environment. But… we need accelerated and achievable blueprints and roadmaps. Even though, an innovative 'never-seen-before' approach might be more interesting and make headlines, our DMAIC approach shows that small process steps can be quite powerful and impactful.

In closing, I want to go back to the insight regarding the extra earning potential with a Six Sigma Green Belt certification. SixSigmaIndy added economic mobility to the strategic 2025 plan. The goal was not just to hope our program graduates earned more money as a result of their new skills, but to facilitate them earning more money. As of today, we are successfully executing on that plan. Because we are the architects, right? It started in December of 2024 with giving two program graduates approximately $3,300 each to rescue a SixSigmaIndy project that did not work out as planned. In June 2025, we were able to bring a cohort 1 graduate over to my for-profit consulting business to help with a contract focus on organizational assessment, effectiveness, communication, culture, and systems. These are the types of projects I really like, but I couldn't do it alone. The budget allows her to make more than $15,000. This means $15,000 extra dollars to her household income. As I write this book, I am transitioning the facilitation of our Six Sigma Yellow Belt Program to three program graduates which help them add more money to their households. The Institute executing on the plan to facilitate increased economic mobility for our program graduates. We cannot count on the system to reward them for the increased skills and greater leadership that they gain from being with us; therefore, we BUILD. Someday, I might go back to the man who clearly had a dislike of nonprofit programs. I think he might be pleased by what we're doing now. On the other hand, I probably won't go back to him. His words motivated me, and I am building what is needed.

Reflection Questions – Chapter 6: Creating the Blueprint – Growing the Institute

1. What systems or routines in your life need improvement or reimagining to support your leadership?

2. What could you build or contribute to building if you had no barriers?

Chapter 7: The DEI Problem

"Creating opportunities for communities within existing power structures often proves problematic, but problematic for whom?"

– Joy E. Mason

Despite increased DEI commitments, it is believed that many DEI programs fail to directly address systemic barriers affecting Black and Latina women. Our goal was to change that percentage, but doing that required us to define "systemic barriers". Systemic barriers are built-in policies, practices, or norms that limit access to opportunities for certain groups. These barriers are not based on feelings; they are based on data and patterns across time, geography, and institutions that consistently show unequal outcomes. These barriers are often invisible, long-standing, and based on factors like race, gender, or income. For example, a workplace that promotes based on informal networks can block qualified individuals, especially women or people of color, from advancing in their careers.

To directly address the barrier of access, we proudly partnered with a local university. It felt like an important step toward our vision, to use Six Sigma to address systemic barriers, provide opportunities, and build equitable leadership. However, sometimes those who start the vision with you will not be the ones who continue the journey with you. Our first university partner ended after one year. I am thankful for their partnership. That university was the right partner at the right time.

However, as I began to ask more questions, the partnership began to crumble. Most of my questions centered on the fact that our participants did not come from the manufacturing sector. Consequently, I suggested that the use of statistical software may not be applicable for our cohort. I asked *a lot* of questions, which challenged the status quo. I was eventually told via e-mail that I was compromising the integrity of the training program. I delayed my response to his e-mail message and reflected. Pause and reflection allowed God to take the wheel because in that moment, I was angry. I found his word choices condescending and triggering.

Shortly after the email message, a key constituent quietly leveraged his resources and without fanfare, opened the door to a different university partner, which lasted for three years. Why did the second partnership end? It ended because we chose to support those who are too often mentored less, sponsored less, promoted less, and paid less than their peers. Unless data has become a banned word, we chose to let the data drive us. The data says……most Black women lead their households. So when their pay is inequitable, it's not just their futures at stake– it's the futures of the children they are raising. For these women, even higher education doesn't close the gap, degrees don't open the same doors compared to their peers. The system isn't just unequal; it's stubbornly resistant to the very progress it claims to value. That's why intentional support isn't preferential treatment; it's long-overdue correction.

The university wanted a broader focus. But their version of inclusion avoided the uncomfortable truth, that those most impacted by inequity are often Black and Latina women. And when you start prioritizing those who've been systematically pushed to the edges, you shake the foundation of the status quo, and that bold shift must continue. So, the Institute continues to center the work on those who experience the least opportunity and the fewest legacy benefits. We choose to acknowledge that opportunity gaps are not equally distributed. We choose to stay true to our mission. And in doing so, we created something even stronger: a program unafraid to name the problem and work toward real solutions.

Let me be clear though: neither race nor gender are selection criteria to participate in the Six Sigma Green Belt certification cohort program. What matters here is the applicant's commitment to building blueprints for equitable opportunities, allowing data to be a powerful guide and creating solutions that uplift and empower others. Under the June 29, 2023, Supreme Court rulings- *Students for Fair Admissions v. President and Fellows of Harvard College* ("SFFA v. Harvard") and *Students for Fair Admissions v. University of North Carolina* ("SFFA v. UNC") – we are permitted to ask about applicants' lived experiences (race or gender). That insight matters—not to exclude, but to understand the full depth of each person's journey and how those hard-earned insights can help dismantle barriers, reshape systems, and open doors for others. Their lived experiences are the blueprint's foundation.

> **"We are permitted to ask about applicants' lived experiences (race or gender). That insight matters – not to exclude, but to understand the full depth of each person's journey."**

Our lived experiences include:

- **Pay Inequity**: Black, Latina and Native American women are paid less than white men and white women for the same work, even with similar education and experience levels.

- **Promotion Gaps**: Women are often overlooked for leadership roles due to bias in promotion practices that favor those within dominant networks.

- **Occupational segregation**: Native American women are overrepresented in low-wage frontline roles (e.g. janitors, healthcare aides).

- **Bias in Hiring**: Resumes with "Black-sounding" names are less likely to receive callbacks, regardless of qualifications.

- **Fewer High-Level Opportunities**: Women are underrepresented in executive leadership, boardrooms, and high-paying industries like tech and finance.

- **Lack of Social Capital**: Structural exclusion from elite educational institutions and professional networks hinders access to career-shaping opportunities.

These are not isolated incidents. They reveal systemic patterns that stifle advancement, despite women's talent and qualifications. In fact, these patterns are antithetical to merit, excellence, and innovation (MEI). We don't want a handout or another round of three-letter acronyms. We want the opportunities we've earned.

So the Institute chooses to focus on opportunities. Regardless of the terms used, what we're really confronting–especially now–is the discomfort of naming injustice while still demanding change. "DEI" is an acronym that didn't even exist a decade ago, so the acronym itself doesn't matter. What matters is fair opportunity. In today's climate, we are fighting not just for opportunity, but for civil rights that should never have been up for debate or compromise. And let's be clear, Black people's fight for justice and opportunity has always been a fight for ALL people. For example, the U.S. civil rights movement not only dismantled legal segregation but also led to broader labor protections, anti-discrimination laws, and social programs that improved education, housing, and employment opportunities for working-class White Americans as well.[5] These are the types of blueprints that work.

Back to the university partnership…….. the end of that relationship freed us. It gave us the opportunity to align with funders, partners, and participants who truly believe in equity—not as a buzzword, but as a practice. It also allowed us to untether ourselves from institutions that saw us as a liability. When we divorced from the university, I went to work bolstering our curriculum and adding more structure to seek accreditation elsewhere. In March 2025, we submitted our package to the world's largest Six Sigma accrediting body. By June, we earned full accreditation; proof that the "divorce" wasn't a setback, but a setup for something greater. As we say in church, "Won't He do it?" While the completeness and quality of the submission definitely mattered, it was the mindset of self-efficacy, determination, and confidence that undergirded this significant milestone.

We serve unapologetically. We serve strategically. And most importantly, we serve with the full understanding that equitable opportunities are not given; they are built and expanded by those bold enough to lead. We are the architects of the systems we're looking for.

---

[5] Katznelson, I. (2005). When Affirmative Action Was White: An Untold History of Racial Inequality in Twentieth-Century America. W.W. Norton & Company.

Reflection Questions – Chapter 7: The DEI Problem

1. Where have you felt pressure to dilute your truth in order to be accepted?

2. What would it look like for you to lead with integrity, even if it costs you something?

3. How has your lived experience actually been the blueprint for something?

Chapter 8: The Transformation Of Women Leaders

"When a woman transforms, she doesn't just find her power, she multiplies it in others."

– Joy E. Mason

Transformation is a word that's easy to say, but hard to measure – until you see it happen right in front of you. I've watched women walk into our Institute with their voices softened by years of being overlooked, their confidence damaged by negative stereotypes, and their dreams filed away in mental folders labeled "someday." And I've watched those same women finish the program standing tall, speaking boldly, and advocating not only for themselves, but for their teams and communities. They've learned to advocate with stories from their lived experiences, like they always have, in combination with data analyzed through the lens of a powerful framework. That's what transformation looks like at our Institute, not just new skills, but new mindsets and confidence.

Leadership is not always about position or title; it's about presence, clarity, and courage. In our program, many women realize for the first time that they've always been leaders. They learn to analyze systems, solve problems with qualitative and quantitative data, and drive measurable results and they start to recognize how to add more executive value. And when a woman recognizes her value, everything changes: how she speaks in meetings, how she negotiates opportunities, and how she leads others. She shows up differently.

One story that always stays with me is of a participant who, during the program, started questioning her role at work. She had been doing more than what her job description outlined, leading teams, improving processes, mentoring others, but she never thought of it as leadership. Through coaching and project work, her confidence increased. A few months after completing the program, she negotiated a higher-paying role in a new department and later became a mentor for the next cohort. That's the ripple effect of transformation, when women rise, they pull others up with them. A zero-sum game and win-lose mentality *is not* the truth of who we are.

We intentionally frame Six Sigma as a tool for leadership, not just a set of technical steps. Every step in the *Define, Measure, Analyze, Improve, Control* model mirrors the journey of leading change. Leaders must define the problem with clarity, measure what matters, analyze root causes instead of symptoms, improve with intention, and build structures to sustain success. Our participants don't just learn Six Sigma, they embody it. And that embodiment shows up in how they approach everything, from team meetings to community initiatives.

> **"In a society that too often asks Black women to settle, sacrifice, or shrink, our institute becomes a space where they are invited to expand."**

Another shift I've seen is emotional: women begin to give themselves permission to dream again. In a society that too often asks us to settle, sacrifice, or shrink, our Institute becomes a space where they are invited to expand. We create environments that feel both rigorous and nurturing—places where excellence and grace coexist. And in that balance, women find the confidence to reimagine what leadership can look like, not just for themselves but for those who follow them.

What surprises many participants is how their transformation impacts others. One woman told me her teenage daughter started sitting in on our Zoom sessions because she wanted to "learn what Mom was learning." Another said her project team at work now sees her as a go-to person for navigating tough challenges. These women don't just shift within the program, they shift in their homes, workplaces, and circles of influence. Their growth is visible, tangible, and contagious.

If there's one thing I've learned from leading this work, it's this: When we are given the right tools, we don't just participate, we lead. And when we lead, we do so with vision, integrity, and community at the center. That is the transformation we witness at the Institute. And that is the kind of leadership our world desperately needs.

You don't have to take our word for it. Here's what some of our alumni said:

"Completing the SixSigmaIndy Green Belt program has been an incredible journey of growth and learning. I'm grateful for the opportunity to gain valuable technical skills while addressing inequities and making a meaningful impact in the community. This experience has not only enhanced my ability to incorporate equity into process improvement but also deepened my commitment to driving positive change in both my workplace and beyond."

"Thank you for this life-changing opportunity. I look forward to using my new skills in my professional and personal life. This program is something special and will continue to affect positive change in the community and in the lives of the women who have this experience."

"I appreciate the opportunity to be part of this cohort, as it has encouraged me to do

things outside of my shell. I am thankful for the opportunity, because in the work I am doing, I am able to implement tools to implement the process that will allow us to further reach our goals."

"Joy has put together an amazing team of talented, professional trainers, coaches and advocates of whom provided excellent preparation and consistent support. I am grateful for the opportunity to have been a member of this cohort. I had the ability to work with some really smart women, who also are passionate about ensuring equity is advanced for those of historically marginalized communities. The skillset I have acquired has already allowed me to better approach my work from a process improvement lens and has broadened my understanding and application of systems thinking."

"I'll speak from breaking barriers as a first aspect, having a data-driven approach just with the Six Sigma, it empowered me to advocate for equity in a way that resonated within my organization. It helped to build credibility and I would say recognition as well. Another way is advocacy for inclusion. So my training enabled me to strategically address the lack of engagement among our educators of color within the union. And so I tackled those challenges by demonstrating how the data could highlight those disparities with effective solutions. I will also say resilience. You know, as a Black woman, I face bias, but Six Sigma provided me with that framework to help focus on measurable outcomes, which helps shift the conversations from personal challenges to the benefits of inclusion and again, data-driven policies. Those were ways for me to break those barriers, advocacies and resilience. I forgot to share earlier too when I started with the Association in May, I was in salary negotiations. Having the Six Sigma certification did help along with other things in terms of the salary negotiation."

"I never really considered how a business improvement approach could impact me personally. So I decided to test his theory and see if I could apply them to my life. And so at that time, I was working in state government. I had been there nearly 20 years and I was just 'comfortable'. That's when I knew I wanted to explore other *opportunities, but I was kind of weighed down with self-doubt. So I just never really ventured out of that comfort zone. I hadn't finished my undergraduate degree. I convinced myself I was too old to go back to school and that it was just too late for me to make any big changes. But the Green Belt training actually pushed me to approach my life with the same strategy I would to solve a problem at work. Using those tools in my personal life helped me realize that the same strategies we used to improve processes at work can be just as meaningful and change your life."*

Reflection Questions – Chapter 8: The Transformation of Women Leaders

1. How has your environment shaped your leadership—and is it time to reshape that environment?

2. What version of yourself are you becoming when you start to fully believe in your own brilliance?

Chapter 9: Community, Connection, and Confidence

"It's all connected: the waiting and the work."

– Joy E. Mason

At the Institute, we teach tools, frameworks and strategies, but one of the most powerful outcomes is something less technical and more soulful: community. We don't just build resumes here; we build relationships. Our cohorts aren't just classmates; they become co-strategists, sister circles, and lifelong sources of support. That network has become one of the most potent byproducts of the Institute experience.

In many professional settings, Black and Brown women are isolated, often the "only one" at the table, in the room, or on the team. I recall being the only one in 4-H and my Girl Scouts troop; I was the only one in most of my high school classes at North Central High School in Indianapolis; I was the only one in almost all of my classes at Miami University in Oxford, Ohio; I was the only one in my graduate classes at Butler University in Indianapolis; and I was the only one in an exempt position in the Dry Products division at Lilly. In almost all spaces, I was different. I was different not just based on skin color, but my family was different. I grew up in an activist household, a household that fought for civil rights for the least of us. That isolation from being the only one can erode confidence.

Isolation and being perceived as different due to race, gender, ability, or background, profoundly affect one's identity, confidence, and self-worth. These experiences often lead to stereotype threat, where individuals fear confirming negative stereotypes about their social group. This fear doesn't just undermine performance; it can also drive people to overcompensate, working tirelessly in an effort to prove they are not the stereotype.[6] This relentless striving often comes at the cost of mental and physical well-being, as individuals internalize the pressure to represent their entire group. Over time, this dynamic erodes authentic self-expression and fosters a constant sense of being judged or on display. It's a strange feeling of feeling invisible and hyper-visible at the same time. The result is not only a fractured sense of belonging, but a silent crisis of identity and mental well-being that often goes unseen.

When I reflect upon my mother's confidence, oftentimes she would reflect on the deep confidence she carried from attending an all-Black school, where her classmates looked like her and her teachers were Black and brilliant. The confidence was not necessarily about Black people teaching Black people. My mother and her classmates were nurtured. Their teachers believed in their greatness, and that belief was mutual. Expectations were high, and the students rose, not out of fear, but out of pride. Yes, segregation pressed in from all sides, but inside those classroom walls, the weight of doubt melted away. They weren't the "only ones." They were seen. They were safe. They were a community.

Many times, I've tried to imagine what it feels like to walk into a room where the people who truly hold power look like you, speak like you, and share your values. A space where your very presence is affirmed, not questioned. Where who you are is reflected in both the spoken words and the unspoken norms. Where your culture, your cadence, and your confidence are not exceptions, but expectations. That kind of room builds more than connection, it builds connection AND social capital to thrive and to rise.

---

[6] Steele, C. M., & Aronson, J. (1995). Stereotype threat and the intellectual test performance of African Americans. Journal of Personality and Social Psychology, 69(5), 797–811. https://doi.org/10.1037/0022-3514.69.5.797

At our Institute, we try to build community, connection and confidence. You walk into a room filled with powerful, soulful human beings who reverberate the same energy and care about the same kind of impact. Let's talk about our energy. Our energy is fueled by an eclectic mix of pain and purpose, passion and righteous anger, resilience born from struggle, joy reclaimed, and creativity that dances, sings, shouts and cries.

That collective energy and courageous spirit is sacred and generational. It transforms the learning space into a safe space where, as Frankie Beverly sings, Joy and pain are accepted as one, and the anger is not judged; it's actually embraced as a spiritual launch pad for growth. What is a safe space? Safe spaces are places where we can show up as our full selves without fear of direct or indirect judgment, punishment, or harm. It's the ability to speak, lead, question, make mistakes, or express raw emotion without being labeled as "angry," "aggressive," "unqualified," or "too much." The Institute is safe.

Safe spaces relieve us from the need to be hypervigilant. Safe spaces bring us relief that we could show up without code-switching or over-explaining. One woman said, "This is the first time I've ever been in a professional space where I felt seen." That kind of affirmation doesn't just feel good, it's spiritual fuel. It gives them the strength to be bold when they return to spaces that are oftentimes unsafe.

The connections forged inside our Institute have grown into something bigger than our sessions. Alumni share job opportunities, recommend each other for opportunities, and even launch businesses together. They create a social capital ecosystem, one rooted in reciprocity and intentionality. That's especially critical in communities where access to generational wealth and institutional power is limited. As I've said in workshops and interviews, social capital, not merit, is the currency that creates mobility. And our Institute helps our women build wealth in relationships.

Here are a few examples:

One program graduate established a very positive relationship with her external team over the course of the six-month project. The relationship was so positive, she applied for and got a job with that same organization. Of course she was qualified, but the relationship mattered. Relationships always matter.

Another program graduate leveraged her relationship with a graduate from a later cohort to get a job at a nonprofit agency. The graduate who has been working at the agency for about two years advocated for her Six Sigma sister. Of course the graduate was qualified: she was more than qualified, but relationships matter.

> *"In a world that asked us to shrink, we built a room where women could finally take up space-and call it holy."*

Another program graduate was desperate to leave her employer because of a horrible attack by a man who must've had mental health issues. Her urgent desire to leave wasn't about the organization necessarily: it was about the trauma inflicted by the unprovoked attack by an angry donor. Shortly after the graduate shared her situation with me, an open position managing community partnerships was brought to my attention. I forwarded that position to the program graduate the morning applications were due. She applied and was quickly notified of an interview date. There were over 200 applicants. Her qualifications got her that interview, but it was the Six Sigma sisterhood that notified her about the opportunity.

In today's environment, there is a lot of discussion about merit over diversity, equity, and inclusion. These discussions knowingly or unknowingly pretend that merit is the primary qualifier. When it comes to opportunities, relationships and connections matter. They always have. It's called social capital.

Social capital refers to the value and benefits that come from relationships, networks, and trust among people and groups. It's the idea that connections between individuals and organizations can be used to solve problems, create opportunities, and build stronger communities or systems. Social capital is what helps people help each other, and we choose to build our own social capital.

It's not just about who you know, it's about how you show up, how you support others, and how you leverage those relationships for *collective* gain. That mindset shift is a game changer. Participants begin to see that networking isn't transactional, it's transformational. And when done well, it creates space not only for individual growth, but also for community-level impact.

Confidence is often born in a community. When you see another woman negotiate a higher salary, launch her own consultancy, or present her project with poise, you start to believe you can do the same. Confidence is contagious. And within our Institute, that confidence multiplies. It's in the way participants carry themselves, speak up during sessions, and reimagine their future. It's not bravado; it's belief. It's not egotistical; it's a deep reclamation of the power He gave us. We are fearfully and wonderfully made!

This chapter of the Institute's impact is deeply personal to me. I've spent years navigating systems that weren't built for us, often feeling like I had to over-perform just to be seen. Now, through the Institute, I get to build something different, something rooted in collaboration and empowerment. Our community is not just an outcome of the work. It *is* the work. And it is one of the greatest joys of my life to witness what happens when we are given the space to connect, uplift, and soar together.

Reflection Questions - Chapter 9: Community, Connection, and Confidence

1. Do you have a circle that truly sees, supports, and stretches you—and if not, how can you build one?

2. How are you building your social capital?

3. How are you helping to build the social capital of others?

Chapter 10: Using Every Talent – A Biblical Reflection

"You were entrusted with talents not to bury, but to build."

– Joy E. Mason

The Parable of the Talents has always resonated with me. In the story, a master entrusts his servants with talents (valuable resources) before leaving on a journey. Two out of three servants invested those talents and multiplied them. The third servant buried his talent. When the master returned, he asked each servant what they had done with their talents. To the first two servants, he said "Well done, good and faithful servant. You have been faithful over a little; I will set you over much". However, the master discovered that the third servant, out of fear, buried his talent in the ground. The master scolded the one who played it safe.

I've returned to that story often, especially when I've felt tired, uncertain, or discouraged. It reminds me that the gifts we're given aren't meant to be buried. They're meant to be used, stretched, and multiplied.

That parable wasn't just a sermon, it became a blueprint for how I live and lead. Every skill I developed at Lilly, every painful experience I survived, and every dream I dared to pursue has been a talent. And I've made it my mission to use all of them, not just for my own success, but for the collective good. What good are my talents, if:

I hoard them

I turn my back on where I came from or

I die with my talents unshared.

I will not ignore others, I will not forget where I came from, and I will not die with my talents buried and unshared.

Founding the Institute was not just a professional goal; It was a spiritual assignment. A way to put all my talents to work in service of something bigger than me.

I remember praying for clarity in the early days of the Institute. But the more I sat with it, the more I felt that this was my assignment. And with every challenge, I was reminded: God doesn't call the qualified, He qualifies the called. I was equipped not just by training and experience, but by faith. Faith that said, "Keep going. Use what you've been given." Even when I didn't feel ready, I moved anyway. Faith walks faster than fear.

> **"Faith walks faster than fear."**

There's a kind of holy pressure that comes with knowing your gifts are needed. I couldn't waste time wondering if people would understand the vision. I had to start building. And as I built, God kept sending confirmation – women showing up, funders believing, impact multiplying. I realized I wasn't just leading an institute. I was stewarding a movement. And every time I saw a woman walk away from our program more confident, more strategic, more powerful, I felt that spiritual alignment all over again.

This is what I believe: our talents are divine. They're not just things we're good at – they're tools we're called to use. And using them doesn't always mean big stages or high visibility. Sometimes it means showing up for a cohort call after a hard day. Sometimes it means helping one woman believe in herself again. Sometimes it means sharing a difficult truth in love. The real reward isn't applause, it's alignment. It's knowing that your gifts are doing what they were designed to do: change lives.

Over the years, I've learned that faith isn't passive. It's active. It's the quiet decision to say yes, again and again, even when the road is unclear. It's the ability to forgive oneself for small and large mistakes and embarrassing missteps. I've had my share of both. It's trusting that your talents, your story, your scars, your skillset can be used for good. That's why I continue to write, to speak, to mentor, and to build. Not because it's easy, but because I refuse to bury what I've been given.

To every woman reading this who's questioning her worth or wondering if her gifts matter: they do. You don't need permission to use them. You don't need to wait until you feel "ready." Your talents were never meant to be stored away, they were meant to shine. And when you offer them boldly, faithfully, and consistently, you're not just making a difference. You're honoring the One who gave them to you in the first place.

Reflection Questions – Chapter 10: Using Every Talent – A Biblical Reflection

1. What talents have you buried out of fear, perfectionism, or past disappointment?

2. What would it look like to live in a way that fully honors every gift God has given you?

Chapter 11: Trials And Triumphs – Leading Through Storms

"Storms don't stop leaders – they reveal them."

– Joy E. Mason

In 2018, three years before launching the Institute, I received a brain tumor diagnosis that froze time. At that moment, everything around me went still. The world didn't stop, but it no longer made sense. The news was surreal, as if I had been dropped into someone else's story. Thankfully, the tumor wasn't growing, so we adopted a watch-and-wait approach. For two years, I lived in the space between normalcy and uncertainty, attending annual visits with a neurosurgeon and a neuro-ophthalmologist, praying and holding my breath each time for good news.

Before every appointment, I underwent MRIs with contrast, those long, echoing scans that are as emotional as they are medical. The contrast dye injected into my bloodstream helped the doctors see the tumor more clearly. It highlighted what shouldn't be there, the tumor's size, shape, and position. It showed them whether it had shifted, grown, or pressed too close to something vital. But for me, it revealed something else entirely: the thin line between peace and fear.

Even now, when I visit the hospital for a mammogram, which is also located in Radiology, I tense up when I hear the steady, mechanical drumbeat of the MRI machine just down the hall. The sounds pull me back to those quiet, heavy moments, lying flat in a surgical gown, breathing slowly, deliberately, eyes closed, praying for stillness in my soul. I would whisper to myself, *"God's got me. Breathe. Breathe. Just breathe."* This was my mantra. Without it, I would've had a full-blown anxiety attack.

Then came 2021. One appointment changed everything. My neuro-ophthalmologist confirmed what my spirit already knew: the peripheral vision in my left eye was slowly shrinking. The tumor was growing, pressing against my optic nerve, stealing pieces of my sight and forcing me to confront a hidden fear. It was no longer safe to wait. The MRI schedule changed from once a year to every six months. Even as my body was fighting a quiet battle, with Denola's steady support, the Institute didn't miss a beat.

My neurosurgeon still wasn't recommending surgery, but my father and step-mother recommended that I get a second opinion. That's when we turned to the Mayo Clinic in Rochester, Minnesota. I researched and found a team of experts who specialized in tumors like mine. Within 30 days, I met with three Mayo specialists. Their conclusion was clear and urgent; have surgery to remove the tumor as soon as possible. The scans revealed the tumor had wrapped itself around my pituitary gland and the optic nerve. If we waited for too long, it could take the vision from my right eye, too.

Tony and I didn't panic, but we were numb – mixed with a new sense of urgency. Regarding the Institute, I had a choice to make: would I step back or slow down? Or would I trust, truly trust, that everything would be okay? I chose to lead through it. Not because I had no fear, but because my faith was my safety net and my family was my rock.

We scheduled the surgery for right after the Cohort 3 project launch, July 8, 2022. I poured my heart into that launch, knowing it might be the last thing I'd see clearly with both eyes. Denola and I facilitated the project launch meeting to lay the groundwork for their six-month journey and then I quietly disappeared. I didn't tell the cohort I was leaving for brain surgery in a few weeks, but I left detailed instructions with Denola for keeping family and friends informed, for keeping my consultants paid, and to keep the cohort going.

Tony and I made the trip to Rochester with quiet courage and heavy prayers. The Mayo Clinic was everything we hoped for, skilled, thorough, and compassionate, but checking in for brain surgery still felt unreal. It's one thing to talk about tumors and treatment plans; it's another to lie in a hospital bed, sign consent forms and say goodbye to life as I knew it, even if only temporarily. I remember the chill of the hospital gown, the sterile smell of the room, and the way Tony lovingly held my hand as if he was anchoring me to this world. Tony's touch always calms me.

The surgery lasted twelve long hours. I don't remember waking up, not at first. But Tony, always by my side, captured a moment in his cell phone that I hold close to this day. While still heavily sedated, I sang, "*When you believe in the power of God, no matter what, special things happen.*" My words were slurred, my eyes were still closed, but the praise was real. Even in that foggy in-between space, my spirit reached for gratitude. I made it through the surgery. I was still here.

As the anesthesia wore off and the fog lifted, something became heartbreakingly clear; I couldn't see out of my left eye. Different doctors came in and out of the room asking me if I could see out of my left eye. Each time, the answer was the same: no. Tony became increasingly agitated by their questions, because it was clear that I couldn't see. Immediately after surgery, the medical team asked me if I could see out of my left eye, and I responded yes even though I was heavily sedated. However, the optic nerve apparently had a stroke shortly after surgery. The very thing they tried to protect (my eyesight) was lost. And yet... I made it. I was alive. I could breathe, speak, move, and feel the love of my family by my side.

Losing my vision in one eye was a painful blow, but it didn't break me. I had faced the storm, gone under the knife, and returned changed, but not defeated. I read somewhere that blindness is one of the top things that people fear. My faith didn't protect me from losing sight in one eye, but it carried me through it. Tony and my family also carried me through it.

Over the two weeks we stayed in a hotel near the hospital so the doctors could closely monitor my recovery, there were moments when I quietly broke down. I would whisper through tears, "I can't see," grieving what had been lost. But Tony, with unwavering love, would lean in and whisper back, "You *can* see." His words weren't just about my vision, they were about hope, perspective, and all the things I still had. During that time, I was surrounded by an incredible circle of love, my mom, stepdad, sister, our oldest son, dad, stepmom, my cousin, and even my mentor. Their presence was a steady light in a dark and uncertain time. What a profound blessing it was to be held by family, to be reminded I wasn't walking this path alone.

Tony was so thoughtful as he always was. Over a ten-day period starting in the hospital, Tony bought me three seven-inch-tall ceramic, elegant angels. He bought them one at a time and each had a message. The first Angel held her hands in prayer; her name was Faith. The second Angel crossed her arms across her chest, and her name was Love. And the last Angel he purchased was named Hope. Her arms were clasped against her heart. Faith, Hope, and Love. I had them all. *"And now these three remain: faith, hope and love. But the greatest of these is love." 1 Corinthians 13:13*

The next few months were focused on recovery at home.

Unfortunately, more storms came. While I was still healing from surgery, one of our sons faced a serious health crisis. We found ourselves speaking to several doctors again, this time not for me, but for him, asking hard questions, making painful decisions, and trying to stay encouraged through months of uncertainty. Just as we found our footing and got him somewhat settled, our other son was a victim of a tragic and deadly fire that resulted in him having serious burns from head to toe. The site of his tearful eyes through layers of gauze was painful. He was in so much pain. Miles had to be taken back to surgery for debridement, the painful but necessary process of scraping away burned and dead skin so the body can begin to heal. It's done under anesthesia, but as a mother, I couldn't stop thinking about what it must have felt like for him afterward. The rawness, the shock to his system, the confusion of waking up in even more pain than before. My heart ached imagining his skin, already wounded, being scraped in the name of healing. I sat there helpless, holding on to faith, wishing I could carry some of the pain for him. Thank God he is still with us. Thank God.

As if that wasn't enough, there was one more storm to come. The final blow, my cousin, only 40 years old, passed away without warning. When Tony told me he died, it was a moment I'll never forget. Tony picked me up from work – we were down to one car, and I had gone back to work. As soon as I got into the car, he turned to me with gentle eyes and said the words, "Brian is dead." I was stunned. I opened the car door, stepped out of the car, stumbled a few steps and collapsed into the grassy patch behind the parking lot. My knees gave out. The tears came hard and fast, and I cried from a place so deep, I didn't know it existed. Tony and one of the Six Sigma Black Belt coaches were down on the ground with me, holding me as I sobbed uncontrollably.

That was the moment I broke. For the first time through all the storms, my surgery, the partial blindness, our son's health crisis, our second son's tragic fire, our stepdad's illness and now Brian's sudden death, I asked a question I had never dared to ask: *"Why, God? Why?"* My cousin was only 40. He was my paternal aunt's only son. He was loving and he was funny. At any family gathering, we could count on him to lift our spirits with his humor. He could've been a stand-up comedian. He also took care of my aunt, his mother. Whatever she needed, he was there. Brian's death wasn't just another heartbreak; it was the weight that finally shattered my spirit and stripped me of the strength I had been clinging to. Through my deep sobs, I cried and asked *"Why Brian? Why has all this happened? Why Brian? Why, why? How much more can we take?"*

My family went through a lot within a short period of time. Each tragedy had left its mark – a mark that hurts when we pause in the quiet moments. Yet somehow, somehow.... through the reflection and the pain, I continued to lead a growing movement that was calling women to rise, even as I was struggling to stand myself.

In those moments, I had to redefine what strength looked like. It wasn't about being stoic or pushing through. It was about learning to ask for help, to rest when needed, and to find grace in the middle of chaos. I leaned on my team, my mentors, my husband Tony, and most importantly, my faith. There were days when I wrote follow-up emails through tears. Not because I wanted to prove anything, but because I couldn't bear to let the vision stop growing. The women we served were counting on us.

> **"I am not superwoman. I try to be super faithful."**

What surprised me most was how the Institute became a place of healing, not just for others, but for me. When I was in pain, I found peace in purpose. When I felt uncertain, I found stability in systems. When I doubted my strength, I saw it mirrored in the resilience of the women we were empowering. Each cohort reminded me why I started. Their breakthroughs became my own. Their wins reminded me that even in the darkness, light was being birthed. I've said it before and I'll say it again: I am not Superwoman.

I try to be super faithful. I believe I was created to lead–even in the valleys. That belief has been my compass through every storm. It's what kept me grounded when the world felt like it was spinning. And it's what has allowed me to hold space for others while also holding space for myself.

The Leadership needed to build blueprints is not about perfection– it's about perseverance. It's about leading through the storm, not in spite of it. The Institute didn't pause while I healed; it evolved. And so did I. Every trial shaped me. Every triumph reminded me that purpose doesn't always come wrapped in ease. Sometimes, it comes through fire. And when it does, we emerge not just stronger, but more committed than ever to the work that calls us.

Reflection Questions – Chapter 11: Trials and Triumphs – Leading Through Storms

1. What storm have you survived that actually strengthened your leadership muscle?

2. Where are you still trying to lead through pain instead of from purpose?

Chapter 12: We Are The Architects – Reimagining Workforce Development

"We are not waiting for permission to build."

– Joy E. Mason

The questions are no longer just, How do we get a job? How do we create work that matters in a future that's already here? Apprenticeships are being praised as the new golden ticket, modeled after systems like Switzerland's. And while there's merit in that model of blending on-the-job learning with classroom instruction, our communities must look deeper. The ground beneath us is shifting too fast. We don't just need a program; we need a paradigm shift.

"It estimates that 40% of all working hours could be impacted by large language models (LLMs) such as ChatGPT-4".[7] While this significantly opens the door for human creativity and innovation, it is also the beginning of enormous workforce disruption. Vocational jobs–cashiers, administrative assistants, clerks, assembly line workers, and even some health tech roles –are at risk. AI can already draft legal memos, design logos, edit videos, respond to customer inquiries, and even offer therapy. If you're thinking a welding or clerical apprenticeship guarantees job security for the next two decades, think again. The future isn't just coming, it's already rewriting the job descriptions.

---

[7] Accenture. *A New Era of Generative AI for Everyone*. 2023. Available at: https://www.accenture.com/content/dam/accenture/final/accenture-com/document/Accenture-A-New-Era-of-Generative-AI-for-Everyone.pdf

I've seen this shift firsthand. In my own work, I used to rely on an executive assistant to create training slides, write follow-up emails, organize social media campaigns, and manage my online presence. Now, with the help of AI tools, I can produce a week's worth of those deliverables in under an hour. What I can't outsource is discernment, strategy, relationship-building, or the ability to solve a problem when the solution isn't obvious. That's what we need now. That's what the workforce of the future will need.

So I reflected: What can SixSigmaIndy do now to ensure our participants are ready for the workforce of the future. We can focus on Foundational skills – skills that don't expire or get replaced by the next AI upgrade. Skills like:

- Leadership: Ability to guide, influence, and inspire others toward achieving common goals.

- Critical Thinking and Problem-Solving: Identify problems, think through them clearly, and use structured approaches to find effective solutions.

- Analytical and Creative Thinking: Use both logic and creativity to find practical, innovative solutions within a structured method like DMAIC (define, measure, analyze, improve, and control).

- Technological Adaptability: Use digital tools to improve learning, problem-solving, and decision-making.

- Process Thinking: Understand workflows (processes), where bottlenecks exist, and how to improve step-by-step processes.

- Systems Thinking: Understand how parts of a system connect and apply the full DMAIC process to guide change.

- Data-Driven Decision-Making: Use numbers and facts to make better decisions and show whether a change really works.

- Change Management: Help others adapt to new ways of working by building support, reducing resistance, and communicating clearly.

- Inclusive Leadership: Include diverse voices, build collaboration, and create solutions that benefit everyone.

- Project Management and Quality Execution: Plan and organize work so that tasks get done well, on time, and with input from the right people.

- Self-Efficacy and Resilience: Keep going when challenges come up, stay focused, and believe in your ability to complete tasks.

- Navigating Team Resistance: Recognize when team members resist change and understand how to respond in a way that helps move the group forward.

- Measuring Success: Set clear goals and use specific indicators to track whether success is being achieved.

- Balancing Quality and Speed: Deliver good work quickly by knowing when to slow down for accuracy and when to move fast.

- Prioritization During Competing Priorities: Make wise decisions about what to focus on when multiple tasks or demands are competing for your attention.

These are the muscles we must strengthen in ourselves and our communities. We need to move from task-doers to solution-creators. From job-seekers to architects. I believe our program participants can stretch all the muscles in this list, even when many of them may not believe it themselves.

Let's stop waiting on politicians – many of whom are decades behind the curve and don't have the data, insight, or urgency to design a workforce strategy that centers our people and catapults us economically. Let's face it: our current economic conditions are linked to legislative policies. "America's middle class has been shrinking for the past 50 years. While middle class Americans remain the biggest income group by number of people, the same can't be said of the aggregate income earned by them. Between 1970 and 2021, the share of U.S. aggregate income earned by the middle class shrunk from formerly 62% to just 42%. At the same time, aggregate earnings by those considered high income increased from 29% to 50%. This is despite the fact that the growing high income class is still less than half as big as the middle class in America."[8] They are not helping communities - they are hurting them, especially women leading single-earner households. This chapter is not focused on politics – it's about truth-telling and the architecture needed for economic mobility. We must have a sense of urgency.

What if we decided that *we* are the architects of opportunity, future jobs, and wealth-building?

That's exactly what I chose. God didn't just give me a career: He gave me a calling. He placed in me the skill to build an institute that teaches problem solving as a means of self-reliance, leadership, workforce development, and economic power. I stopped waiting for a solution. And now, I teach others to do the same.

> *"What if you and your community gathered your gifts, your frustrations, your brilliance, and your experiences; and designed a different kind of apprenticeship? One built not just on trades but on transformation."*

---

[8] Katharina Buchholz. "How America's Middle Class Is Shrinking [Infographic]." *Forbes*, April 21, 2023. Available at: https://www.forbes.com/sites/katharinabuchholz/2023/04/21/how-americas-middle-class-is-shrinking-infographic/

What if you stopped waiting, too?

What if you and your community gathered your gifts, your frustrations, your brilliance, and your experiences, and designed a different kind of apprenticeship? One built not just on trades but on transformation. One where students would learn to improve a broken process, resolve conflict, redesign a customer journey, or challenge a systemic injustice. What if they learned not only to work hard, but how to also lead with analysis?

I volunteered for a school in April of 2025 for career day. For about 40 students, we worked on creating an app for social media safety and another app for surviving school. They didn't have computers, so I had them use notecards to document what would be on each app screen. They weren't learning to be web designers; that day; they became architects for solving their own problems. With some guidance, they created the blueprint based on what they knew, without any judgment on what they didn't know. Instead of 30 minutes of showing them how to creatively solve their own problems, what if complex problem solving were embedded throughout the curriculum, even without computers?

We must build our own solutions based on what works. We already know what works.

Have we built the current solutions or did someone else build them for us?

Too many solutions are not working for us or our children.

Let's build workforce solutions that work for *us*.

Workforce models built by us, for us, and with the future in mind. Models where we're not preparing to keep up with change, we're shaping it.

Let's reframe the question:

What does it look like to train our communities to be builders of change, not just survivors of it?

If you're still waiting for permission, this is it.

You are the architect. Build something that lasts.

Reflection Questions - Chapter 12: We are the Architects

1. If you were the architect for a new workforce development model for your community, what foundational skills would you prioritize and why.

2. In a world where you can no longer wait on politicians or one year grants, what is one goal that you could take on to help young people in your community build the skills to solve problems and lead.

3. If you have chosen to be an architect, how can you build faster, bolder and with more urgency?

Chapter 13: Built To Last – Our Blueprint Forward

"Movements rooted in truth, purpose, and people don't crumble; they endure."

– Joy E. Mason

When I reflect on everything we've built through the Institute, one word rises to the top: **blueprint**. Not the kind tucked inside an office drawer, but the kind we've designed over generations, under pressure, in plain sight, and often without credit. Long before equity became a buzzword or data became a demand, our communities were creating roadmaps for survival, strategy, and brilliance. **We are the blueprint.**

Women have always built in the face of opposition. We built education systems when we weren't allowed in schools. We built businesses when banks denied us capital. We built movements, families, churches, and cultural empires – with clarity and purpose. Whether the world acknowledged it or not, **we have been the architects of progress.**

Think of Sarah Boone, who reimagined the ironing board. Or Dr. Patricia Bath, who developed laser eye surgery. Or Phillis Wheatley, who published poetry when Black literacy was considered a threat. Or MaVynee Betsch, the "Beach Lady," who preserved environmental history long before "climate justice" was a phrase. These women didn't wait for permission to innovate – they created the blueprint and dared the world to follow.

In every field, **music, medicine, art, science, academia**, we've shaped the foundation. Mary Jackson and Katherine Johnson didn't just calculate flight paths for NASA. They rerouted history. Kimora Hudson entered college at 12, reminding us that genius has no age limit. From the cotton fields to the Senate floor, Black women have designed systems and solutions that shifted the world.

Now, through SixSigmaIndy, we're not starting something new – we're continuing something sacred. The blueprint didn't begin with us, but we've taken up the pen. We've refined it with Six Sigma tools. We've aligned it with spiritual truth. And we've built it through every cohort, every project, and every brave decision to believe in what's possible.

One of the greatest lessons along the way has been about pace. In the beginning, I sprinted, driven by urgency and vision. But blueprints require patience, precision, and process. I had to accept that greatness is not rushed. Now we build with intention – cohort by cohort, project by project.

We've also learned that alignment is everything. When we lost partnerships because we refused to water down our focus, it wasn't a loss, it was a clarifier. We are not here to conform. We are here to build, and what we are building is for those who have always been told to wait their turn. We're done waiting. We're designing new rooms, new systems, new futures.

Looking ahead, our blueprint expands with purpose. We're reaching into new cities and scaling with purpose. We're not just tracking change, we're making it measurable. Even as we grow, we stay rooted in truth: Black and Brown women are not new to strategy.

Legacy once felt like a final destination. Now, I know it's a living draft. A process. A blueprint. One that others can follow, build upon, and personalize. What we've created is durable, adaptable, and built to last, because it was *built by us*.

So we press forward, not just with dreams, but with designs. Not just with hopes, but with habits. At the Institute, we are not reacting to change; we are engineering it. And we do it in honor of every woman who built before us, every woman building now, and every girl who doesn't yet know she holds the blueprint in her hands.

> *"We are not reacting to change; we are engineering it."*

Now, as you prepare to lead forward, here is your **Blueprint Built By Us**, six steps to anchor your next bold move:

1. Define Your Power

Name the brilliance, story, and strengths you bring into every room. What you carry is not an accident—it's inherited. As you define it, name your fire - the fire in your belly, the fire in your soul. My fire has always burned for justice— and that fire is my fuel. I used to hide that fire, and it would sometimes erupt in not-so-good ways. But now, I embrace it. I own it. My story, my strengths, and my fire are built into my goals.

> *I will use my gifts fully and boldly to create lasting impact in every space I enter. I will also take strategic risks to fulfill this mission.*

2. Measure What Matters

Identify what success looks like for *you*, not for your title, employer, or critics. Success could be the journey itself, especially when we are unsure of the ultimate destination. If this is true for you, you can still be intentional about the steps of the journey. Research and benchmark. It is highly likely that someone, somewhere, is doing something similar. Build off what you find. Combine your goal, the problem, research, your unique value proposition and the context of this moment into a new "thing" that will take you —and our communities— forward. Track all of this and your journey in a journal. Track who you talk to, where you go, what excites you, and what triggers you. Track your pivots, ahas and next steps. Step by step and measure by measure, with a dose of faith, the needle moves and the plans become clearer.

> *I retired at the age of 50 by applying these steps : defining and embracing my power (my fire) and measuring (documenting) my journey and the vision.*

3. Analyze the Barriers

Get honest about what's been holding you back: low confidence, disorganization, fear, unresolved trauma, old narratives that no longer fit, or a group of friends that are now holding you back. Then trace it to the root. Insightful analysis may require spiritual support, therapy, journaling, reading or a trusted friend. In some cases, you may need all of those things!

My analysis revealed:

- **Perfectionism**:
  My analysis revealed old narratives about perfectionism, stories that made me believe I had to get everything right to be worthy. I now realize that striving to be perfect kept (and sometimes keeps) me from showing up as my full, authentic self.

- **Introversion**:
  It exposed how I once saw my introversion as a weakness. But now I honor it as a quiet strength that allows me to listen deeply, think critically, and lead with intention.

- **Acceptance**:
  I uncovered the way I used to chase acceptance in spaces that were never meant for me. Today, I recognize acceptance starts from within.

- **Approval**:
  There was a time when I equated approval with safety and success. But I've learned that constantly seeking validation from others only delayed my own growth and freedom. God approved me at birth.

- **Belonging**:
  Belonging once felt like something I had to earn by shrinking parts of who I was. Now I understand that the only belonging that matters cannot be lost.

- **Triggers**:
  My triggers still have power unfortunately. I acknowledge my triggers are part of my healing and my growth. I give myself more grace by recognizing my triggers may push my buttons and take me breath but it is only temporary. Your barriers don't have to stop you, but the barriers can motivate you.

4. Improve Your Systems

Small tweaks build momentum. Whether it's setting boundaries, reworking your routines, or delegating, choose what makes you more efficient and whole. You can make small tweaks everyday–even every hour. Remember, the devil is working every second whispering softly (and sometimes loudly): "you can't" and "you shouldn't." *Do the thing.* Take a chance. Put yourself out there, with no regrets. Too often I see women who won't take the chance… **NOW**.

They won't choose to heal…**now**

They won't pursue the promotion…. **now.**

They won't start their own business…. **now.**

They won't write the book… **now.**

They won't start the podcast…. **now.**

They won't ask for help…**now.**

They won't take the lead… **now.**

They won't build the " thing" **now.**

Whatever it is…do "the thing" now. It doesn't have to be a big thing, but take a small step now. Life is too short to keep waiting. Create your 30-, 60-, and 90-day plan…now.

> *I left corporate. I started the business. I started a nonprofit. I wrote the book – because I recognize the time is NOW. The brain tumor reinforced the urgency of now.*

5. Control the Narrative

Decide what story you want your life, work, and leadership to tell. Speak it. Believe it. Embody it. *Own your narrative, like your favorite playlist before a big day. You don't let anyone else hit shuffle or choose the vibe.* Your narrative is your positive affirmation.

A 2016 study found that self-affirmations activate the brain's reward system, particularly the ventromedial prefrontal cortex, which is associated with positive valuation and self-related processing. This suggests that positive affirmations can help people respond more effectively to threats or stress, improving their overall emotional resilience and well-being.[9]

> *I play songs like "It's My Time" by Kelly Price or "Joy" by the Georgia Mass Choir. Make sure every part of your leadership*

---

[9] Cascio, C. N., O'Donnell, M. B., Tinney, F. J., Lieberman, M. D., Taylor, S. E., Strecher, V. J., & Falk, E. B. (2016). *Self-affirmation activates brain systems associated with self-related processing and reward and is reinforced by future orientation.* Social Cognitive and Affective Neuroscience, 11(4), 621–629. https://doi.org/10.1093/scan/nsv136

speaks in your voice, your rhythm, your truth. Own your song.

6. Rebuild in Community

No blueprint is executed alone. Let us remember *Ubuntu*, **"I am because we are."** The work ahead isn't just about power, process or promotion, it's about people. It's about choosing connection over competition, and compassion over critique. The blueprint we're building is not a solo act. It's a collective design, forged in sisterhood and sustained by unity. The judgment, based on skin color, zip code, being a single mother, citizenship, or sexual identity, is getting really old. Dysfunctional or divisive narratives about yourself or others are not helpful. You are not better. You are not worse. *I am because we are.*

Our blueprint legacy won't just be measured by process, programs or paychecks, it will be seen in **how we treat the "others."** How we speak to one another. How we honor one another's humanity. How we show up for someone who's different from us. Because how we treat each other is the clearest reflection of how we feel about ourselves. It reveals whether we truly love ourselves, or whether we've quietly bought into *someone else's* narrative of who we are.

Let's get back to the truth of who we are: resilient, brilliant, generous, sacred. The blueprint doesn't have to be complicated.

This is what we build. This is how we rise. This is what makes our blueprint worthy of passing down. Built by us. For us. With us. And always, through love.

Know this…

You were never meant to shrink.

You were never meant to lead alone.

You were *Built By Us*, and you are building what's next *For Us… now.*

Be the Architect.

Reflection Questions – Chapter 13: Built to Last – Our Blueprint Forward

1. Where have you forgotten that you are the blueprint—and how can you reclaim that truth?

2. What bold design are you being called to draft, refine, or complete?

3. How can you honor the blueprint creators before you by building forward with faith and strategy?

Appendix

Every problem holds a blueprint for progress, and in Six Sigma, that blueprint is DMAIC: *Define, Measure, Analyze, Improve, and Control.* The project summaries that follow show how this method isn't just about data, it's about transformation. Sometimes, progress came from small, strategic tweaks. Other times, bold changes closed wide gaps. But in every case, these teams used the power of process to move from frustration to flow, from stuck to solution.

All of the project teams were led by SixSigmaIndy participants in partnership with their clients. Their goal was to improve systems that impacted more than just their gender, race and ethnicity. Their goal was to be leaders and architects of something better.

These stories prove that whether the steps are big or small, when we follow a thoughtful blueprint, breakthrough is possible. *(Names and project details were removed or changed to protect the anonymity of our clients.)*

Project Name: Supplier Diversity: Contract Approval

Challenge

Vendors were not paid in a timely manner, sometimes exceeding 90 days. Late payments disproportionately impacted diverse vendors who typically have less capital to withstand payment delays. **Goal:** Reduce requisition processing time by one month—or 30%—within five months.

Summary:

This project used the six Sigma DMAIC blueprint to uncover the delays that prohibited timely payment of vendors. A key part of the DMAIC method is process mapping. The process mapping for this project revealed an excessive number of reviews and approvals required for a vendor requisition payment. The process mapping process also revealed that one department accounted for the majority of the delays. After identifying root causes, the team recommended direct deposits via ACH and elimination of redundant signatures.

Project Results

The project pilot yielded the following results: 69% decrease in average (mean) requisition processing time, and 483 vendors registered for payment via ACH direct deposit. Out of the 483 vendors, 37 Black-owned businesses registered for payment via ACH direct deposit. We highlight these numbers because Black businesses tend to have less capital to endure delayed payments.

Insights

When the project charter was developed, we had a specific interest in late payments for Black businesses. However, the DMAIC blueprint focuses on process. Everyone is impacted by the payment process, but some are impacted more than others when payments are late. The project helped 37 Black owned businesses get paid faster but please note that 446 non-black vendors will also get paid faster.

This important point is what anti-DEI people often miss. Well-designed DEI programs, when focused on processes and systems, tend to help more than just the people who are marginalized. As the old saying goes, "A rising tide lifts all boats." This diversity supplier project was a perfect example of how we can all rise with the right blueprint.

Call-to-Action

To create smoother systems and faster results, organizations must commit to building processes that are both efficient and effective – starting with a mindset shift. This call-to-action outlines five clear steps to improve operations, especially in procurement and accounts payable. It includes a commitment to paying vendors on time—many of whom are small businesses supporting families and local communities. By using data, mapping current workflows, and applying the DMAIC blueprint, leaders can uncover root causes, test solutions, and build systems that are sustainable and equitable.

1. Commit to efficient and effective processes within all departments, including procurement and accounts payable departments. Efficiency and effectiveness begins with a mindset and the mindset fuels the blueprint.
2. Disaggregate existing data to better understand where the problem is happening, to what extent it is happening, and who is impacted the most.
3. Use the DMAIC blueprint to map the requisition or payment process. Identify the critical steps that are impacting timely payments and root causes for delays. (Based on our project experience, we have found that redundant and unnecessary reviews and approvals were the primary contributors to payment delays).
4. Brainstorm solutions, prioritize solutions and implement solutions in the form of a pilot.
5. Review the pilot results, and refine the solution, build solutions into systems so they are sustainable. …Example solutions could be IT payment systems that only require one procurement reviewer, one quality assurance reviewer and one management approved.

Project Name: Blacks in Tech: Removing Barriers, Reclaiming Possibilities

Challenge

Black job seekers lacked access, encouragement, and confidence to explore careers in tech. Many didn't know where to look, felt they didn't belong, or didn't see themselves represented.

Goal

Help Black job seekers confidently explore and apply for tech jobs by improving awareness, tools, and support at the start of their job search.

Summary

This project used the Six Sigma DMAIC method to uncover barriers keeping Black job seekers from considering careers in tech. Surveys and interviews showed fear, low awareness, and lack of role models. Many didn't apply for tech jobs because they thought they weren't qualified or didn't see people like them in tech roles. The team designed new ways to introduce tech early in the job search. They created a Tech Careers Packet with job boards, starter roles, skill checklists, and salary maps. They also shared a simple "70% Rule", if you match 70% of the job description, go for it. The packet was added to the onboarding process for job seekers. Community partners helped test the solution. Participants were also taught to link their personal skills to tech jobs. The process now includes surveys, reminders, and tracking to keep improving.

Project Results

- Quantitative: 100% of program participants applied to at least one tech job after receiving the new materials.
- Qualitative: Participants said the new resources made tech feel "doable" and gave them the courage to try something new.

Our sample size may have been small, but our DMAIC approach has the potential to increase the number of Black people applying for tech jobs.

100% applied and that's a start…. Applying!

Insights

- Representation matters. Black job seekers need to see others like them in tech to believe they belong there.

- Gatekeeping hurts growth. Systems that limit access, like rigid recruiting practices, must be redesigned with inclusion in mind.

- Confidence is key. Equipping individuals with the language, tools, and support can spark interest in tech careers they may never have imagined for themselves.

Call-to-Action

Tech careers are not just for "others." Tech careers can be a pathway to stability, creativity, and generational change. This project shows that when we design and lead our own system–from workforce training to entrepreneurship, we reclaim power and possibility. We stop waiting for inclusion and start building blueprints that work for us. Blueprints that are data-driven, sustainable, and rooted in equitable opportunities.

60-Day Action Steps for Organizations:

- Step 1: Are tech careers even mentioned in spaces where marginalized groups frequent? Businesses, schools and agencies should talk about tech jobs in all spaces to increase exposure.

- Step 2: Provide Tech Careers Packets (include job boards, starter jobs, and success stories from Black and female professionals) to job seekers.

- Step 3: Teach the 70% (or less) Rule—don't wait for perfection to apply. Too many of us falsely believe that we have to meet all of the job qualifications. That is simply not true. The confidence to apply matters!

- Step 4: Start tracking which job seekers apply for tech jobs and why.

- Step 5: Host one listening session to hear from Black and female job seekers about their fears and interests.

Why it matters:

Taking these steps helps remove fear, spark new confidence, and expand the economic options for marginalized communities. When we build processes *by us and for us*, we create futures where everyone has a chance to thrive.

Project Name: Saving Mothers: A Six Sigma Approach to Maternal Health

Challenge

Black women in Anonymous County were dying at significantly higher rates from pregnancy-related causes compared to white women. A program was funded to implement interventions to increase maternal health and reduce maternal deaths.

Goal

Reduce preventable maternal deaths by improving communication, follow-up care, and timely action across the maternal health program.

Summary

This project applied Six Sigma methodology to confront the crisis of Black maternal deaths in Anonymous County. Across the state, Black women were more likely to die within one year postpartum. The team conducted a detailed review of care processes. A review of statewide data revealed that women who die after childbirth, die within two windows: 1-6 days and 43-365 days postpartum. Even though the program intervention team's participants had exceptionally low maternal mortality, the intervention was 4-6 weeks postpartum, which was clearly after the first high risk period for mothers. The team identified that an intervention prior to this first critical timepoint had lifesaving potential.

Insights

- System delays can be deadly. Timely care and intervention must be driven by data.

- Listening to mothers improves care. Involving mothers in care design leads to better outcomes.

Call-to-Action

- We must stop expecting the most vulnerable women to survive broken systems. We must build better ones—together. The *Built By Us Blueprint* proves that when we redesign systems with our voices, data, and lived experiences, we can save lives.

60-Day Action Plan for Entities with a Similar Challenge:

- Step 1: Map the postpartum care process. Identify the delays, drop-offs, or blind spots.

- Step 2: Interview at least 20 mothers about their care experience, ask what felt missing or harmful.

- Step 3: Create or update follow-up protocols to include mental health and chronic care outreach.

- Step 4: Set a goal: every mother gets a follow-up within a specific number of days **informed by local and statewide data.**

- Step 5: Implement a reliable tracking system with data integrity and frequent monitoring

Why This Matters:

This call to action helps Black mothers feel "safe, seen, and supported"--not just during birth, but long after. It also builds a system where data is valued not just for collection, but for the patterns it reveals and the lives it can save.

Project Name: Work Ready: Opening Career Doors for Fathers

Challenge

Many men, especially returning citizens and fathers, faced delays and unclear steps when trying to access job training and employment support. This led to frustration, missed opportunities, and longer times without work.

Goal

Create a smoother, faster, and more supportive process to connect these men to employment programs that match their skills and goals.

Process Name

Employment Readiness and Referral Intake Process

Summary

This project focused on fixing the agency's process that connects fathers and returning citizens to employment help. The Six Sigma team used our DMAIC blueprint to study the agency's low employment rate. They found issues like missing information and poor tracking of employment partners. As a result, the team created a spreadsheet to track employer information. The spreadsheet was designed to ensure mission alignment and better job matching to the agency's clients.

Project Results

- The new spreadsheet became a critical part of the employer partnership process. Better alignment with and tracking of employment partners should lead to more jobs for clients.

Four Insights

- Black men face unique hiring barriers. Systems and processes must be built with their needs and realities in mind.

- It's better to have only a few employment partners that align with the needs of participants than to have many partners that do not align.

- Memorandums of Understanding that describe roles, responsibilities, and expectations between the agency and the employment partner are critical to success.

- Strategically matching men who are eager to support their families with the right employers and resources within a specified timeframe builds trust and better results. They need to earn money now versus later.

Call-to-Action (Built By Us Blueprint)

Black men deserve systems that work the first time. Too often, they face barriers built into structures that were never designed with them or for them. But when we build with intention, when we center their dignity, brilliance, and leadership, we create more than opportunity, we create transformation. The DMAIC Blueprint reminds us that when Black men work, lead, and thrive, entire families benefit. Communities stabilize. Economies grow.

60-Day Action Plan for Agencies Facing Similar Challenges:

- Step 1: Map your process for identifying employment partners.

- Step 2: Create or improve the process for ensuring opportunities provided by employers match the skills and career goals of clients.

- Step 3: Use templates to cultivate, align, and track employment partners consistently.

- Step 4: Assign a follow-up lead who checks in with each employer regularly–from the memorandum of understanding through six months after the employer hires the client.

- Step 5: Routinely review outcomes and gather feedback from both participants and employers, use that feedback to improve your process. In the continuous improvement world we call this plan, do, check and act.

Note: Managing the employment partner process is a critical component for success–especially for clients seeking a fresh start and aiming to support their families. Clients do not need to be perfect or have all the right skills if the employment partners are selected strategically, thoughtfully and promptly, with a strong focus on what the clients say they want and need.

Acknowledgements

This book is the product of deep faith, hard work, and divine timing – but I did not walk this journey alone.

To my loving husband, Tony: Thank you for being my constant. Your unwavering love, patience, and encouragement have sustained me through every late-night writing session, every cohort, and every storm. You have been my sounding board, my covering, and my calm. Your quiet strength and steady support made this book, and this movement, possible. I love you endlessly.

To my publisher: Your belief in this message and in my voice has been a gift. Thank you for helping me bring this vision into the world with excellence and clarity. Your guidance, trust, partnership and friendship have meant the world to me.

To the women of the SixSigmaIndy: You are the heartbeat of this work. Thank you for showing up fully, for trusting the process, and for allowing me to walk alongside you. You are leaders, pioneers, and legacy builders. This book is as much yours as it is mine. Believe that you are architects.

To my mentors, friends, and fellow visionaries: Thank you for your wisdom, prayers, and gentle nudges. Thank you for reminding me that the road may be hard, but it is holy. Your words and presence have been sacred fuel.

To the village, past and present, that shaped me: Thank you for planting seeds of leadership, excellence, and faith. I carry your lessons in every room I enter.

And most of all, to God: Thank You for the vision, the voice, and the validation. May everything I've built point back to You. Amen.

About The Author

J**oy E. Mason** is a visionary leader, author, and founder of SixSigmaIndy, a transformative program that empowers women to become confident, data-driven leaders who drive equity in their organizations and communities. A certified Six Sigma Black Belt and former corporate executive with over three decades at Eli Lilly, Joy has turned her passion for problem solving into a life-changing platform for economic mobility and leadership development.

But Joy's story is more than credentials. She is a brain tumor survivor, a mother who has led through personal heartbreak, and a woman of unshakable faith. Her journey is marked by resilience, clarity of purpose, and an unwavering belief in the brilliance of those often overlooked.

With grace and grit, Joy has mentored and certified over 100 women, helping them rise in influence, income, and impact.

Through her writing, speaking, and training, Joy continues to inspire women across the country to use every gift they've been given, boldly, faithfully, and unapologetically. She lives in Indianapolis with her husband, Tony, and finds daily joy in serving others, building legacy, and lifting as she climbs.

Index Of Terms

Change Management – A structured approach to transitioning individuals, teams, and organizations from a current state to a desired future state.

DMAIC – A core Six Sigma methodology that stands for Define, Measure, Analyze, Improve, and Control. It is used to improve existing processes.

Equity – Fairness and justice in access, opportunity, and advancement, particularly for historically marginalized groups.

Imposter Syndrome – A psychological pattern in which individuals doubt their skills, talents, or accomplishments and fear being exposed as a fraud.

Mentor – A more experienced person who offers guidance, wisdom, and encouragement to someone with less experience.

Process Improvement – A methodology for identifying, analyzing, and improving existing business processes to optimize performance.

Project Charter – A formal document that defines a project's scope, objectives, stakeholders, and key deliverables.

Six Sigma – A data-driven methodology aimed at improving business processes by reducing variability and eliminating defects.

Social Capital – The networks, relationships, and social connections that enable individuals to advance personally or professionally.

Strategic Thinking – The ability to analyze situations, anticipate future challenges, and plan effectively to reach long-term goals.

Systems Thinking – An approach to problem solving that views complex entities as interconnected wholes rather than isolated parts.

White Belt / Green Belt / Black Belt (Six Sigma) – Levels of Six Sigma certification indicating increasing expertise and responsibility in process improvement methods.

Workforce Equity – The practice of ensuring fairness in hiring, development, compensation, and advancement within a workplace.

SIXSIGMAINDY

SixSigmaIndy was born from a bold vision—to create a place where women could reclaim their power, sharpen their skills, and step into leadership with confidence. What began as a local idea has grown into a movement that equips women with Six Sigma tools, faith in their own voice, and the courage to solve problems that others thought were too big. At SixSigmaIndy, transformation is not just possible—it's expected.

This institute is more than training; it's a circle of support. Women are surrounded by mentors who have walked the same path, coaches who believe in their potential, and nonprofit partners who open the door for real-world impact. Together, participants learn to lean on data, lean on each other, and lean into the strength of their own story. They leave not only as problem solvers but as changemakers, ready to use their gifts for something greater.

The ripple effect is powerful. Women graduate with promotions, salary increases, and newfound influence. Nonprofits gain lasting solutions to persistent challenges. Communities see hope where systems once failed. SixSigmaIndy proves that when women rise with the right tools and the right circle, they build more than careers—they build legacies.

For more information about SixSigmaIndy, visit our website: www.SixSigmaIndy.org.

www.ingramcontent.com/pod-product-compliance
Lightning Source LLC
Chambersburg PA
CBHW051946160426
43198CB00013B/2318